W9-ANN-714

CONTENTS

In 1958 U.S. gross domestic product totaled $485 billion and the economy employed about 14 million manufacturing workers. Now, almost 50 years later the gross domestic product has grown to more than $12 trillion, while manufacturing jobs continue dropping — to about 14 million workers.

One American industry is expected to lose more than 68 percent of its manufacturing jobs to foreign competitors by 2012.

American small towns are being gutted by the record imports of goods and the resulting export of jobs. Hospitals, schools, and government services are struggling in the economic wreckage.

The loss of manufacturing threatens America's research and development industries and the advancement of science.

Some of America's largest "trading partners" illegally manipulate their currencies to make their products unfairly cheap — by as much as 40 percent — while making U.S. goods unfairly expensive — by an additional 40 percent.

Steeling America's Future

A CEO's Call to Arms to Save U.S. Manufacturing

Dan DiMicco

Vox Populi Publishers, LLC
100 North Tryon Street, Suite 4700
Charlotte, NC 28202-4003

10 9 8 7 6 5 4 3 2 1

ISBN 978-0-9790178-1-0
ISBN 978-0-9790178-2-7

Printed in the United States of America.

Some of America's largest "trading partners" illegally use their tax systems to give their products a significant, unfair advantage in their domestic markets and in international markets.

The U.S. government's weak trade posture has made the U.S. a "paper tiger" in the global trade arena. Government agencies and U.S. companies alike kow-tow to foreign governments and business — to the detriment of our industries and workers.

American policies and regulations add more than 22 percent to the cost of our products.

We ourselves are holding some of the wrenches being used to dismantle American manufacturing.

But we are taking action, and the American political grass roots is responding with a call for a new direction and a new resolve to restore American manufacturing, its jobs, and its leadership of technological and social advancement. "Made in the U.S.A. still stands for freedom, fair wages, a safe workplace and a clean environment.

On July 4, 1886, Theodore Roosevelt said, "The Declaration of Independence derived its peculiar importance not on account of what America was, but because of what she was to become; she shared with other nations the present, and she yielded to them the past, but it was felt in return that to her, and to her especially, belonged the future. . . . So it is peculiarly incumbent on us to act throughout our lives as to leave our children a heritage, for which we will receive their blessing and not their curse."

viii

DEDICATION

Thanks to my friends and political field advisors Tom Mullikin, Nancy Smith and their team at Moore & Van Allen for their help in preparing this book. Thanks to the leaders of the Metals Service Center Institute, including its board of directors, Bob Weidner and Bill Hickey, who helped focus America's manufacturers on many of the issues raised in this book. Also thanks to the National Association of Manufacturers Domestic Manufacturing Group and its leaders, including Dave Frengel of Penn United, for helping get the truth out there. All proceeds from sales of this book will benefit local charities in the communities across the country where Nucor people live and work.

PREFACE

The thoughts in this brief book are inspired by the achievements and ambitions of American steel workers. During my career they not only have made the world's best steel, they have reinvented the industry during one of its most revolutionary and innovative periods.

I began my career as a metallurgist, where the work of making better steel begins at the microscopic level. Today, as chairman, president and chief executive officer of Nucor Corporation, the world's largest recycler and the second-largest steel manufacturer in the Western Hemisphere, I am concerned about the future of America's entire manufacturing sector. Global politics and domestic policies make it increasingly difficult for companies simply to make things in this country.

The United States is importing hundreds of billions of dollars of goods and exporting millions of manufacturing jobs.

Our nation's prosperity and success have been built on self-reliance in basic industries such as steel; we owe it to our children's children to maintain this standard. However, global trade and international politics are undermining our industrial self-reliance and economic self-determination. We need to renew our national commitment to manufacturing.

Ultimately our cause should be this: That the United States rededicate itself to the ideal of "making things" — whether they be steel, bricks, clothing or computer chips. These are the material goods that bring financial security, health, well-being and purpose to our lives, and that are essential for our economic and national security — which really are one and the same.

I have written this book with my colleagues in mind: the men and women with whom I have shared my career at Nucor. They represent the skills and accomplishments of everyone who works in American manufacturing. For them and for the shrinking number of Americans holding manufacturing jobs, I offer up these few chapters.

I'll be brief. At Nucor we deliberately created an organization with few levels of management and a high degree of involvement by everyone in the company. We are direct, to the point and understandable to everyone in the room. My co-workers have taught me that this works best.

This book is not built on obscure or hard-to-find information. The facts and figures that I use are available to everyone. My aim is simply to deliver a message that can help us to unite in our purpose, see a clear path forward, and make our nation a better place to live and work.

These few chapters are also part of an unprecedented grassroots campaign that Nucor is leading, supporting and encouraging across this country. We are sharing the ideas and concerns of this book with citizens who have answered our invitation by the thousands — joining us at our steel mills, in college gymnasiums, in vacant shopping centers and even at a stock car race track — because they share our growing concern and alarms that America and American Manufacturing must get our house in order.

The problems that confront American manufacturing today are profoundly altering our nation. We must build the solutions from the ground up — the same way we built our nation.

"Making things" is part of the DNA of the USA.

"Made in the USA" doesn't just tell the buyer where the product was made. It stands for much more than that. And it is more than worthy of our untiring efforts.

Dan DiMicco

Steeling America's Future

A CEO's Call to Arms to Save U.S. Manufacturing

CHAPTER 1
SOUND THE ALARM

Let me begin with Paul Revere. Why? Because he was a patriot who acted on the need to deliver an urgent message to a sleeping populace.

On the night of April 18, 1775, Paul Revere mounted a horse and rode through Massachusetts villages to warn local militias that British troops were preparing to march from Boston. Two other patriots joined him, and on that midnight ride their three voices awoke a people to the stirrings of tyranny on their own shores and also to the potential of a great new nation.

The British had organized a secret mission to seize munitions and to capture patriot leaders John Hancock and Sam Adams. The Americans were prepared for this and had arranged to alert the militias. The famous first signal came when two lanterns were hung in the steeple of Old North Church to indicate to Revere and the other riders that the British were coming: "One if by land, two if by sea."

Revere's message, we are told, was to the point: "The British are coming!" But because local patriots and militias had taken stock of their situation and were prepared, his simple message became a compelling call to action.

As a result, the Americans were equipped to safeguard their arms, protect Hancock and Adams, and on the morning of the next day to repel the British at the battles of Lexington and Concord. When they seized control of their destiny they established our birthright as Americans.

If Paul Revere were alive today I would ask him to make a similar ride.

I would ask him to ride past the checkout lines and the automobile showrooms and the trade fairs where American consumers at every level are sleepwalking through a shopping binge of imported goods that has no equal in our history.

I would ask him to ride past the Capitol and the White House where our elected leaders are wrestling with some of the most difficult challenges our nation has ever faced: free trade, fair trade, the flow of wealth and more. Some of our leaders share a sense of urgency, and like the Massachusetts colonists, are prepared to act on a message from a latter day Paul Revere. Others are not prepared to act on the message.

What message would I ask Paul Revere to deliver today?

Borrowing from his successful first ride I would propose a direct, urgent message that gets to the heart of the matter: "The jobs are going! The jobs are going!"

The jobs in question are the jobs in which Americans make the materials and goods that have built our nation and its economy into the world's strongest. Economists, bankers, politicians and others call it "the manufacturing sector." I call it our nation's traditional economic and cultural backbone.

The questions for Americans are these: If the jobs are indeed going away, where is our future headed? Are we prepared today to hear a message like Paul Revere's — as his long ago compatriots were prepared? Are we prepared to act when the call to arms goes out?

4

Today, entire American communities are being gutted of their factories and mills. Industries that employed generations of families have been shuttered, with the jobs either lost to foreign competitors or exported by American companies trying to stay afloat in a global playing field perverted by cheap labor and unfair and illegal trade practices.

In 2006, American manufacturers employed about 14.2 million workers. That is almost exactly the number of U.S. manufacturing workers in 1958. In that year, our gross domestic product was about $467 billion (in 2006 dollars). By 2005, our gross domestic product had expanded to nearly $13 trillion. Imagine that! An economy of under half a trillion dollars had the same number of manufacturing employees as an economy of more than $12 trillion.

Several factors have led to this anomaly. Our 21st century economy is much more diversified, with many products and services that did not exist back when cars had fins. Also, the manufacturing sector has made huge gains in productivity. Thanks to automation, improved industrial processes, and innovations in every aspect of manufacturing, we are able to create more products using fewer workers.

Half a century ago in the steel industry, for example, the electric arc furnace had never been used for high volume steel production. Today it is the heart of a process that Nucor refined and adapted to a new business model that it brought to the steel industry in the 1960s. This leap in productivity contributed to both the growth of Nucor and the steel industry as a whole. It also enabled us to expand our recycling operations to regions far from the traditional steel cities, which were built close to iron ore and coal.

So when we look at our constant number of manufacturing workers during an exploding economy, is the glass half-empty or half-full?

Some claim the economy is naturally diversifying away from its old dependence on manufacturing. Others state that our gains in productivity and innovation mean that manufacturing is still strong.

But consider this: Less than one decade ago the U.S. economy employed more than 17.7 million people in manufacturing. From 1998 to 2001 we lost almost 2 million workers, and from 2001 to 2005 the number of manufacturing employees plummeted by an additional 1.5 million.

Some of that loss can be chalked up to the recession that struck in the early 2000s. But economists studying the job recovery trends since the recession tell us that our current situation is unlike any since the Great Depression.

I am firmly convinced there's a lot more going on here than just the usual business cycle.

The National Bureau of Economic Research has identified November 2001 as the month when the most recent recession ended. From that point through mid-2003 the economy shed an additional 1.1 million jobs. And unlike previous economic recoveries, the pace of job creation continued to fall even as the economy officially was in "recovery."

What's more, manufacturing industries continued to shed jobs. As a manufacturer, I found it very difficult to talk about the post-recession "recovery" as we continued to shed hundreds of thousands of jobs. And this is not an academic issue for us in the steel industry. And frankly, it is not a Nucor-specific issue because we at Nucor have never laid off employees due to a downturn in business. However, many of our most important customers are also manufacturers or distributors that depend on manufacturers.

Economists point us in many different directions to understand reasons for job loss: business cycle, September 11 economic impacts, high energy costs, and international trade. We should look at all of these factors, but our nation's lack of focused, pro-manufacturing policies in such areas as trade and regulatory burden is adding to the ongoing erosion of manufacturing jobs.

Just as important, I believe something is eroding our confidence as a people in the future of American manufacturing. As a consequence, we lack a willingness to forge strong policies or even to invest in the manufacturing sector.

Studies indicate that the lack of manufacturing job creation in this most recent post-recession recovery period may be linked to reduced investment. Clearly, many potential investors sense that our nation and its elected leaders lack the focus and willpower to create forceful, pro-manufacturing policies and enforce them. With that in mind, it seems perfectly natural that people might invest their money elsewhere — either in another part of the economy or another part of the world.

Likewise, too many of our best and brightest students will focus on careers and disciplines that appear to have more promise. Who will hitch their career wagon to industries whose main incentives and ambitions appear to be headed offshore?

I believe also that something is fundamentally dulling our reactions to what is going on in our own economy. Given the depth and speed of manufacturing job losses in the United States, I am frankly shocked that we have not responded as a nation with greater focus and urgency.

Take Texas for example. Like the United States itself, Texas and its skilled workforce helped invent high-technology manufacturing, creating the products and the manufacturing processes that produced huge economic benefits for our country. Not many years ago, the Texas high-tech industry was a huge economic engine.

In 1992, about 116,000 Texans manufactured computers and so-called "peripherals." By 2000, that number had grown to almost 169,000. But the number of jobs has since tanked to fewer than 112,000.

I think most of us know the standard explanations by heart:

- The tech bubble burst;
- Texans can't compete with low-wage offshore workers; and
- Productivity gains in other locations helped shift the production.

But I hear an alarm sounding.

Maybe it's because Nucor has several facilities in Texas, and I feel a strong bond with the state and its people.

Maybe it's because I know that they are capable of competing with the world's best when it comes to quality and productivity.

Maybe it's because more than 110,000 Texas jobs were lost in manufacturing computers, electronics, peripherals, semiconductors and communications in just over five years.

The U.S. Bureau of Labor Statistics reports that job losses in these industries reflect two major trends: One, we have increased automation and productivity in the manufacturing process and, two, we're importing more of these products than ever before. The Bureau of Labor Statistics projects that these trends will continue, with employment expected to decline by another 12 percent in the computer and electronic manufacturing industry in the decade from 2002 to 2012.

But that 12 percent figure looks positively rosy compared to projections for apparel manufacturing. For years, economists, industry analysts and others have spoken of the decline of U.S. apparel manufacturing as a foregone conclusion. The conventional wisdom has been that a U.S. apparel worker making $9 to $10 per hour cannot compete with a Latin American or Asian counterpart making just 31 cents per hour.

So when the U.S. Bureau of Labor Statistics projects that more than 68 percent of American apparel manufacturing jobs will be lost from 2002 to 2012, this news is greeted with a shrug. We are becoming conditioned to say, "It's inevitable. We can't compete." In round numbers we have just shrugged off another quarter million jobs.

Our attitudes overlook one crucial point: Many of these industries have mounted valiant efforts to survive. In the decade from 1993-2002 the textile industry averaged more than $2 billion per year in capital investment and raised its productivity by 165 percent. But the flood of imports rose relentlessly, and the American Textile Manufacturers Institute worked with only limited success to call attention to the currency manipulation and unfair trade practices that pumped up the foreign exporters like economic steroids.

For years certain pundits and policymakers have been willing to downplay job losses in various manufacturing industries perceived as inherently uncompetitive. Just a few years ago some people in the tech sector shrugged off job losses in the textile or apparel sectors, thinking that those old-time, labor-intensive industries were just inherently ready to have their jobs snatched away, in spite of their massive investments and heroic efforts to compete. Some people also suffered under the illusion, "It can't happen to me."

Some undoubtedly have dismissively looked at earlier job losses in apparel manufacturing and thought, "This job loss will level off after a while."

It's safe to say that we'll begin to see those losses level off during the next few years — after an additional 70 percent of our apparel manufacturing jobs are lost and we approach zero jobs.

The steel industry has been viewed in similar fashion. Business experts of various stripes have continued to position our industry and our workers as inherently vulnerable to offshore competitors.

Nucor's success and growth in the steel industry was built on the foundation of starting with basic products and basic levels of quality and working our way up the value chain. We did not cede volume of any product line to our competitors, including those products at the lower end of the value chain, for this basic reason: Ours is a capital-intensive industry, we require capital to operate and grow, and the growth of our capital required growth in volume.

It is a very misguided notion that industry can survive, let alone thrive, by moving from niche to niche in the marketplace. Certain apologists for the loss of American manufacturing jobs offer vague hopes about manufacturers carving out various niches and becoming specialty or boutique manufacturers, but this is a misguided hope.

In his book, *Good to Great,* author Jim Collins writes about Nucor's success relative to its competitors and makes the point that the best performing companies never vacate the bread and butter for the dessert. Basic goods produced by basic industries such as steel and textiles provide value to the companies that produce them, to their workers, to research and development and to technological progress and innovation. My own company is a living example.

My point is this: We should never be complacent about the loss of any manufacturing jobs!

We should not dismiss the loss of jobs in one manufacturing sector just because it's not our own. There was a time when those of us in the steel industry focused on our own industry and not so much on manufacturing as a whole. That is certainly no longer the case at Nucor, where we are working not just on behalf of steel but on behalf of the entire manufacturing sector. And I am pleased to say that this point of view extends from the board room to the steel mill, for reasons I'll explain later.

We should not shrug off the loss of manufacturing jobs because it seems to be a relatively small number. In the past few years we have become increasingly concerned not only by the number of jobs we've lost but by the speed at which we're losing them. What we have learned is that if external forces are allowed to gather enough momentum and seize enough advantage we can lose jobs and production capacity at a stunning rate.

We should not shrug off the loss of manufacturing jobs because of timid foreign policy or because our standard of living is higher than those of our competitors. United States manufacturing does not exist to transfer wealth or technology to our competitors because they do not match us in wealth or economy. It is one thing to help a needy neighbor; it is quite another thing to hand that neighbor an entire industry on a silver platter.

We should be jealous of every job held by every citizen in our country. And the moment we believe that our jobs are being hijacked by illegal or unfair international practices, we should respond decisively and effectively.

Case in point: China. By now most Americans are aware that "Made in China" has replaced "Made in USA" on many (if not most) of the things we buy. We have huge trade deficits with China, but we have trouble fully tuning in to the endless arguments among economists about whether this will help us or hurt us.

But when it comes to manufacturing jobs in the United States there can be no doubt that the Peoples Republic of China is the 500-pound gorilla sitting in the middle of our living room.

The Economic Policy Institute, in research prepared for the U.S.-China Economic and Security Review Commission, reported that the U.S. trade deficit with China between 1989 and 2003 displaced production that supported 1.5 million jobs. About 75 percent of these were manufacturing jobs, which paid above-average wages.

In the years covered by the study some disturbing trends emerged.

By 2003 the fastest growth in job displacement had shifted to "highly skilled and advanced technology areas once considered relatively immune, such as electronics, computers, and communications equipment." In other words, China began to whittle away at our high-tech productive capacity faster than other industries. So much for the conventional wisdom that the U.S. need only worry about sewing machine operators in t-shirt factories.

As the report stated, "China has moved aggressively up the product ladder from labor-intensive non-durable products (e.g., clothes and shoes), to more sophisticated machinery and durable goods."

As a result, the United States passed an historic milestone in 2002: For the first time, our nation bought more advanced technology from foreign countries than we sold to them. Our trade imbalance with one nation — China — accounts for our entire trade deficit in this crucial and strategic manufacturing sector.

The report also stated that the rate of job displacement due to our trade deficit is accelerating. Since 2001, our growing trade deficit with China has more than doubled our nation's loss of job-supporting production. During the period covered by this study, the overall trade deficit with China grew twenty-fold.

No one is immune; the report indicates that these effects have been felt in all 50 states, and, it is worth noting, in other nations. Here in the U.S., the effects on job creation are staggering. In the areas where we managed to increase exports, enough demand was created to support just under 200,000 jobs. But because our imports from China grew at a very high rate, the production capacity to support almost 1.7 million jobs was lost to Chinese factories. That nets out to 1.5 million jobs lost from our economy to China's booming manufacturing sector.

Why do I start with China?

China's one-party, Communist government has orchestrated a top-down industrial and trade policy that has exploited every loophole and advantage of the global political and economic system while also exploiting a huge work force that is subject to low wages, long hours and few social or economic protections.

The world's ability to construct an effective and fair system of global trade can create big opportunities and big problems because we have to build it at the same time we're trying to make it work. It's like the old example of having to finish building the airplane while it's up in the air.

China is adept at exploiting every advantage. For example, many Chinese companies are owned all or in part by the Chinese government. This can make any enterprise an extension of government policy.

Imagine, for example, that the U.S. government owned significant interests in our country's steel mills. (China's does.) Now imagine that it became an official (if un-announced) policy of the U.S. government to increase our share of the world steel market, or to limit our own market's exposure to competition.

All that our government would need to push forward this agenda is two things: money and power.

In China, the government has a firm grip on both. Within its Communist system the government owns and controls significant portions of that country's means of production. And because it is a one-party state, there are no checks and balances on whatever the government (The Party) decides to do. Chinese government policy is shaped outside the public view, and those outside its power structure see only what the government wants them to see.

For more than a decade, the Chinese government has used that country's currency to carve out an advantage for Chinese-made goods. The practice is called "currency manipulation" and only recently has it attracted interest among the media and political leaders.

As controversy, "currency manipulation" has proved a tough sell to the media. It's hard to make it interesting or understandable in just a few sound bites. But many of us in manufacturing have hammered away at currency mani-pulation and other issues, trying to push them front and center. The good news is that we are making progress. But our efforts have required huge effort and much time. The cost of doing nothing has already proven to be too high. When it comes to unfair trade practices, time is not just money — time is jobs, jobs and more jobs.

And as we are seeing today, it eventually whittles away at our standard of living.

So how can I make "currency manipulation" relevant to the average American? First, I'll tell you that it is costing us our jobs. The job losses I described above can be chalked up in part to currency manipulation.

Second, I'll tell you that it results from the deliberate actions of a foreign government and creates an unfair advantage, or "un-level playing field," as it is called in international trade.

Basically, the Chinese government has kept the value of its currency artificially low relative to the U.S. dollar, which means that our dollars are artificially expensive relative to the Chinese currency, the yuan. China implemented this long-term strategy more than a decade ago, when it initially devalued its currency by more than 80 percent, then pegging its currency's value to the dollar to maintain the advantage.

Here's how Dr. Peter Morici of the University of Maryland summarized the effects of currency manipulation for 2004: "China's currency manipulation creates a subsidy on its exports equal to nearly 9 percent of its gross domestic product and 21 percent of its exports."

So it becomes a "stealth subsidy." And, unlike direct subsidies to particular industries, the government can declare that it has left no fingerprints at the scene of the crime. At the same time the distorted currency values act as a hidden duty, or tax, on American goods, making them more expensive and less competitive within the Chinese market. So currency manipulation greases the skids for China to export goods to the U.S. while making it more difficult for our goods to be sold in Chinese markets. That is not free trade!

China accomplished this advantage for more than a decade by "pegging," or fixing the value of its currency, the yuan, at a certain level relative to the dollar. In a true open market currency values are allowed to "float" or rise and fall in value relative to each other depending on what is happening in the market.

But with China's top-down, one-party rule they were able not only to keep the currency peg in place but have used the full power of the Chinese government to intervene in the currency markets in other ways. Over a period of 6 years the Chinese government engaged in a concerted and growing purchase of dollars to keep upward pressure on the dollar's value relative to the yuan. The purchases grew from about $8 billion in 1999 to more than $134 billion in 2004. At some points during 2005 the purchases approached nearly $1 billion per day. By August 2005 China held $769 billion of our currency in reserve.

The reason for this was simple. Chinese goods were flooding U.S. markets and U.S. dollars were flooding into China. It was the only way China could prop up the value of the dollar. In July 2005, China officially abandoned the peg and "revalued" its currency by about 2 percent — well shy of the 25 to 40 percent distortion of the two currencies' relative values. Although slated to float against a basket of currencies, it is generally understood that the government will maintain the same tight rein on its currency that it keeps on its citizens and its economy.

One under-reported side effect of this has been to reduce the buying power of the Chinese at home. China's own people are less able to purchase the goods they need and to improve their standard of living. But this need is sacrificed on the national altar of exports at any cost.

Even a quick look at the data shows how great the distortion of the currencies has become. The graph below shows the radical adjustment of the Chinese yuan in 1994 and the total lack of market-based adjustments for a decade following. The little uptick in the graph in 2005 reflects the meaningless and insignificant "adjustment" permitted by the Communist government since the currency "revaluation" was announced with much fanfare.

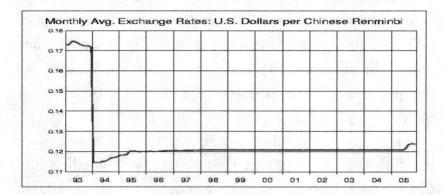

This graph shows how effectively the Chinese government has pegged its currency to the U.S. dollar for more than a decade. No market influences, including the unprecedented and damaging U.S. trade deficits, have been allowed to change the relative values of the currencies.

We fully expect government policy to continue to keep the value of China's goods artificially low, which also keeps Chinese wages depressed and basically has the same effect as a heavy tax on Chinese workers' take-home pay. This helps drive down domestic consumption and further fuels exports. But the Chinese government does not answer to its workers, and it carefully creates every artificial advantage possible in global trade.

Dr. Morici estimates that China's intervention lowers our nation's gross domestic product by as much as $500 billion, displaces higher paying jobs with lower paying jobs, and reduces job creation, wage increases and tax revenues, while increasing budget deficits.

"In the near term," Dr. Morici writes, "consumers enjoy lower prices at discount stores and shopping malls, but the effects on American prosperity and economic leadership are highly corrosive."

As a metallurgist, the term "corrosive" gets my attention. In the world of steel we understand that corrosion attacks metal in several different ways, some of which are easy to detect and others that are not. But anyone who has ever loved a car knows that when corrosion gets to a certain point the car can quickly be reduced to scrap metal and become worthless. There is a fine line of rust between the body shop and the junkyard.

At times I believe that we in the United States are waiting for our economy to "rust through" before we get upset enough to take action. Car lovers know that when the rust eats all the way through it is often too late. The same could be said for our economy in general and our manufacturing sector in particular.

The bad thing about corrosion is that time is never on your side. You can't outwait or outlast corrosion. Trade issues are the same way. The quicker you address the problem the less it is going to cost you.

Let me turn to an example from my own industry. The first point I should make is that this is just one small example of the kinds of disputes, tugs-of-war and challenges that go on every day in international trade. These actions have something for everyone — legal proceedings, political hearings, diplomatic posturing, and scenes that might recall a game of five-card stud in an old Western movie: first one blinks, loses.

Trade disputes can be a grind. But they are a very important grind, and for American manufacturers the outcome can determine profit or loss, survival or bankruptcy.

When it comes to the steel industry we do have some elements of a good novel: ambition and jealousy. Every nation on earth with an ounce of economic ambition wants to establish and maintain a strong steel industry. Those economic ambitions might center on industrial strength or military self-reliance or just to establish a nation's identity as an industrial economy. Whatever the reason, steel is usually fundamental to a nation's economic agenda.

Along with that ambition comes a jealousy of any country or company that threatens that nation's capacity to produce steel. Once established, the steel industry almost always becomes a priority of national politics and economic policy.

As a long-time steel guy naturally I can understand this point of view. We share the belief that steel is essential to economic well-being and self-reliance. Experience also has taught me that it is why you have to keep a sharp eye on every competing government and steel producer.

In March 2005, media attention continued to focus on the war in Iraq and the Michael Jackson trial. Most people probably missed the news about hearings conducted by the U.S. International Trade Commission that dealt with certain "hot-rolled steel products from Brazil, Japan and Russia."

The March 2005 hearings were conducted by the ITC and featured testimony from industry leaders and Congressional representatives. The gist of the testimony and investigations was that steel producers and/or governments in three very different countries — Brazil, Japan and Russia — were engaged in actions that either unfairly subsidized or "dumped" the steel they were exporting to the U.S.

"Dumping" occurs when a product is exported and sold in another country at prices that are less than the cost of production. It often is carried out by steel producers and governments facing excess capacity who don't want to shut down the factories and mills.

The hearings also focused on the question of whether the steel imports from Brazil, Japan and Russia were causing material damage to the U.S. steel industry.

Rep. Melissa Hart of Pennsylvania testified at the hearing, and here is part of what she said: "The U.S. steel industry has been in a state of crisis since the late 1990s. At that time, a massive surge of subsidized and dumped imports from Brazil, Japan and Russia imploded the U.S. market during what should have been the up-side of the business cycle. These imports were dumped in the United States by as much as 185 percent below fair market value."

"In July 2000," Rep. Hart continued, "the U.S. Department of Commerce issued a comprehensive study examining the underlying causes of the crisis confronting the U.S. steel industry. It provided disturbing evidence of collusive activity among foreign producers in the world steel trade. These anticompetitive actions keep foreign markets closed and channel steel to the world's most open market — the United States.

"The study also demonstrated that foreign governments have created vast unnecessary capacity by providing billions in subsidies to their domestic steel companies. These foreign steel companies must export their surplus to maintain capacity utilization."

The hearing was just one chapter in the ongoing story of "Free Trade versus Fair Trade." The principles of "Free Trade" can be summed up in about two pages. The nitty-gritty work of ensuring "Fair Trade" never ends.

In 1999, the U.S. Commerce Department arrived at three separate determinations regarding steel exports from Brazil, Japan and Russia into the United States.

The U.S. investigation determined that starting as early as 1983 and continuing through 1991 the Brazilian government had infused large amounts of money into Brazilian steel producers, basically converting their debt to equity. It would be like Uncle Sam stepping in during the third year of your mortgage and with a stroke of the pen upping your equity in your house to 80 percent. This had the same effect as lowering the companies' cost of doing business or providing a subsidy. Take away the infusion of government money and you take away the ability of the steel producer to sell steel in the U.S. at the lower, or subsidized, price.

About that same time the Commerce Department found that Japanese steel makers were dumping steel into the U.S. market at margins ranging from 17 percent to 40 percent, in round numbers. At that margin below cost it is pretty easy to see what effect this would have on steel prices in the U.S. and our steel producers' competitive position.

But the Japanese couldn't hold a candle to the Russians. Commerce Department investigators determined that the weighted average margin for steel being dumped by Russia into the U.S. market ranged from 74 percent to 185 percent in round numbers. Selling at those margins below cost cannot fail to damage the competition, in this case U.S. manufacturers.

The role of the U.S. Commerce Department and the U.S. International Trade Commission is also to determine if such actions by our trading "partners" can inflict "material injury" on our domestic industry.

In the case of the steel products in question they looked at the metallurgical qualities of the steel, how it was manufactured and whether the steels from Brazil, Japan and Russia could be sold in place of a variety of U.S.-produced steel products. They expended a lot of effort in determining the fine points of the imported steel's impacts on U.S. markets and U.S. steel producers.

Not surprisingly, the U.S. government's investigations found that during the mid-to-late- 1990s, the volume of steel imports from these countries increased. In the merchant market these imports increased their market share to more than 10 percent in 1997 from 4 percent in 1995. This while their prices were dropping, by anywhere from 12 percent to 20 percent.

A key finding was that both Japan and Russia had significant excess steel manufacturing capacity, which positioned them to dump increasing amounts of their product into the U.S. market as they continued to capture more market share.

And the U.S. market was definitely the place to be in the late 1990s. The Asian financial crisis had knocked the wind out of the Asian market, while the U.S. market as a whole was experiencing strong demand and rising steel consumption. In particular, the "hot-rolled" steel in question is a desirable product and market. This is a high-quality steel product that is rolled into sheet steel coils, and which has a variety of uses in a range of manufactured products. It's a quality, value-added steel product that comprises a vital part of the steel producers' product line.

By 1998, the prices of Brazilian, Japanese and Russian steel imports continued to decrease sharply while the import volumes increased. In its findings, the International Trade Commission reported, "The declining prices are especially significant because they coincided with increasing demand for hot-rolled carbon steel products...During such a period of high demand, with the domestic industry operating at a high capacity utilization, prices would not be expected to decline."

Unless the trade in question was unfair.

The U.S. government determined that this was in fact unfair trade and that it could inflict material injury on the domestic market and steel industry. For those reasons, the government took steps to counterbalance the unfair subsidies and dumping of steel at less than fair value.

Under U.S. law and international trade agreements, our country has reserved the right to impose what are called "countervailing duties" and "antidumping measures" to protect the integrity of U.S. markets. Our federal government is entitled to implement these measures and has the accountability to use them to impose duties on unfairly imported products and remove any unfair price advantage of the imports. A countervailing duty can be added to the price of an import to erase the illegal price advantage.

In the case of the Brazilian, Japanese and Russian steel, the U.S. was allowed to impose these measures in 1999 for five years. After that time, the duties either expire ("sunset") or are continued.

Toward the end of that five-year period the Commerce Department conducted a new investigation to determine if the conditions of subsidy and dumping still existed with the countries and producers in question. The ITC convened hearings at which affected and interested parties could testify.

I attended that hearing in March 2005 and offered testimony on behalf of Nucor and U.S. steel producers. From our perspective, the situation regarding steel from Brazil, Japan and Russia had not changed since 1999. Brazil continued to circumvent the duties, and our government failed to protect our markets effectively against the illegal actions. With regard to Russia our government failed to implement a consistent policy by allowing large shipments through a quota agreement. If things had been put right in the three countries' steel industries and governments then, the U.S. market measures could have been allowed to sunset.

But the hearing and the government investigation determined that the potential for dumping, the inherent Brazilian subsidy, and the potential for material damage to the U.S. market all continued. The market protections would continue for another five years.

The investigation of illegal trade practices and the imposition of countervailing duties and antidumping measures is just one small part of the huge effort required to govern global trade. The list of "sunset reviews" conducted by the Commerce Department and International Trade Commission is unbelievably long and diverse. Here is just a small sample:

- Canned Bartlett Pears from Australia
- Large Power Transformers from France
- Extruded Rubber Thread from Malaysia
- Chrome Plated Lugnuts from Taiwan
- Uranium from Uzbekistan.

The entire list would cover several pages. But consider how different these businesses are from each other — the Taiwanese lugnut factory from the Uzbek uranium processor from the Australian pear cannery. Then consider how different the governments of these respective countries are — an Asian Tiger, a former Soviet satellite, and a Western Democracy.

The manufacturers in these diverse cultures and systems of government must all compete with each other, with their domestic rivals and with the inherent bureaucracies and burdens that arise within their own country.

Some companies and some governments are very adept at playing the international trade and geopolitical game. Consider the examples we've looked at so far: Brazil, China, Japan and Russia. In the century just past we fought wars in which China and Japan opposed us. With Russia we engaged in a Cold War in which nuclear weapons and massed armies took brinksmanship to an almost unthinkable level. We've never battled with Brazil, but today Brazil joins these and all nations as our rival in international trade.

One of the crucial questions to be addressed by our nation today is: How do we face these trade rivalries and conduct foreign policy in dealing with trade issues?

As a nation we must awaken to the idea of a global economy, embrace its opportunities and gird ourselves to compete effectively within it. This will require not only the resolve of federal and state officials but also of the American people. American workers and families across the country should be reminded of Daniel Defoe's words to Parliament regarding the right to petition government to address grievances, a right (and responsibility) that is inherent in our system: "Our name is legion and we are many." We need attention and action by the legion Americans and communities who have been hurt by our malaise on these important issues.

The examples of Chinese currency manipulation and steel from Brazil, Japan and Russia show us that there is no one answer, no single political posture or national attitude that will prove effective to each disparate case.

In the case of steel imports we must be methodical and work through the bureaucracy that has been created to resolve trade issues. We gather facts, we build and present our case, and then deal with the outcome. In the example of hot-rolled steel from Brazil, Japan and Russia, the ITC agreed with the U.S. Commerce Department's findings and maintained the market protections for another five years.

The example of currency manipulation with China rises to a different level than the steel example, however.

First, the manipulation of a nation's currency affects its competitive trade position across every industry. An inherent currency advantage can apply to virtually everything you make and sell to other countries.

The difference between the hot-rolled steel issue and currency manipulation issue is like the difference between a cut on your foot and cancer. The cut is a localized injury that you can repair with surgery and direct treatment. Cancer has the potential to damage the entire system and every organ and limb. The treatment must be geared to restoring the health of the whole system.

Currency manipulation must be addressed immediately. The longer we delay in curing the problem the greater the damage.

But in fact our nation's approach to seeking a remedy for currency manipulation has been hesitant and unfocused. We have tried rhetoric, back-slapping and diplomacy. Perhaps we have tried too much carrot and not enough stick. I am no diplomat or international negotiator, but I do know that while the Chinese government deliberately kept its currency pegged and bought up billions of dollars we saw an unprecedented trade gap open up and bury countless American manufacturing jobs.

The actions of the Chinese government with regard to its currency extend back more than a decade. The pace and size of their currency interventions accelerated in the 2000s, when China had become a member of the World Trade Organization.

WTO rules clearly prohibit currency manipulation. Our country unquestionably has the rules on its side and we have suffered damage from this unfair practice — not only in trade with China but with Taiwan, Japan and Korea, which are allies as well as trading partners. These other Asian trading partners have intervened on a massive scale in international currency markets, buying up hundreds of billions of dollars to maintain artificial currency values.

So why have we not confronted the issue swiftly and decisively? Our international trade deficit is completely out of control. Our manufacturing sector has hemorrhaged jobs, and entire industries are being gutted. The very wealth of our nation is flowing into Asia by the hundreds of billions of dollars. Yet, it seems we are not awake to the fact.

I believe that if Paul Revere were alive today he would call us from our sleepwalking and call us to action. He would arouse Americans to lead and to act for our own best interests and the ideals that this nation represents.

I believe this because Revere was not only a patriot he was a pioneering industrialist and manufacturer. He helped establish production of copper plating and copper spikes that were used to plate American warships, including our cherished U.S.S. Constitution. Some of his original brass cast hardware is still part of this ship. He was an accomplished businessman and a technological innovator in metal rolling technology. More than 200 years ago he recognized that the United States' national defense and security depended on our ability to manufacture basic goods and materials. As a steelmaker I can't help but feel a strong kinship with this famous patriot.

In 2005, the company that bears his name joined with Nucor to help awaken Americans to the threats that imperil our manufacturing and our national security. Mr. Brian O'Shaughnessy, President and Chief Executive Officer of Revere Copper Products Inc. joined with us and thousands of New Yorkers at a town hall meeting in support of manufacturers.

Mr. O'Shaughnessy spoke urgently and forcefully to a gathering of citizens who had come out on a chilly, rainy night to hear about unfair trade practices and other urgent concerns of American manufacturers.

Paul Revere would have felt right at home at this town hall meeting, and I believe he would have been proud that the company that bears his name is home to patriots and citizens who care enough to call us to action.

It is time to awaken the resolve and energies of Americans across the country to these important issues. The time has arrived for action. If we are to make any kind of future for our country and our children we must continue to make things.

CHAPTER 2
THE VALUES BEHIND "MADE IN THE USA"

Nations, governments, economic systems, and societies work in fundamentally different ways, and they result in very different circumstances and conditions for their people. One of the big corporate and marketing buzzwords of recent years is "branding." The concept is that a company's brand is established by every characteristic, quality and trait of the company's products and services. People may associate different qualities with a company. One company may be known for low prices (positive) and also low wages (less than positive). Both of these traits will in some way define the corporate "brand." Another may be known for top quality goods but at a premium price. Another company's name and brand may be built around sustained financial growth, and another's built around world-class customer service.

In today's global marketplace nations also get branded in the arena of public opinion.

It is important for us to take stock of our national brand, particularly with regard to the products that are stamped "Made in the USA." What does this mean?

It means one heck of a lot.

Welded into the American way of doing business are certain fundamental values, beliefs and social commitments that define us as a people. When we stamp, sew, solder, emboss, affix, glue or tattoo "Made in the USA" on a product, it stands for our nation and our people — who we are, what we are and what we stand for.

Does "Made in China" stand for the same thing? I don't believe it does. Part of the reason lies in how the USA arrived where it is today, compared to China, and part of the reason lies in where we are going in the future.

When we study history, civics and American government we typically learn about founding documents such as the U.S. Constitution and the Declaration of Independence.

Similar milestone documents in our history have fundamentally shaped our business, industry and culture. We don't usually learn about them in school, but given the "no-holds-barred" rules of global markets, perhaps we should.

Let me give you some examples.

"The Fair Labor Standards Act of 1938" does not have the same ring to it as "The Emancipation Proclamation," but it is part of the fabric of American business and our social contract. It advanced values and standards that we take for granted today.

The U.S. Congress enacted this legislation to create labor conditions that would promote the "health, efficiency and general well-being of workers."

Note that Congress wanted to produce benefits for both workers and industry. The benefit for workers is health and well-being. The benefit for business and industry is efficiency. The Act stated that the lack of fair labor standards:

- Burdens commerce and the free flow of goods;
- Constitutes an unfair method of competition in commerce;

- Leads to labor disputes burdening and obstructing commerce and the free flow of goods; and
- Interferes with the orderly and fair marketing of goods and commerce.

The premise was simple: if your system of industry and trade lacks fundamental labor standards then the system will suffer from unfair competition, labor disputes and a lack of order in the marketplace.

The Fair Labor Standards Act imposed the minimum wage. Americans as a whole probably don't give this much thought today. It is an accepted part of the landscape. Our businesses and elected officials give it a great deal of thought, every time the political debate resumes about whether to increase the federal minimum wage. But for U.S. workers as a whole it is a part of the social contract that we expect to see continue.

This legislation was instrumental in codifying such cornerstones of our culture as the 40-hour work week, overtime pay, compensatory or "comp" time, and child labor protections. It's also significant to note that the fair labor standards extend protections not just at the factory floor or place of employment but also through the selling and shipping of goods. That is, if you violate the wage and hour provisions while producing goods it could be a further violation as you sell and ship those goods. The legislation did not turn a blind eye to unfair labor practices' effects beyond the factory.

When we are honestly able to stamp a product with "Made in the USA," the label stands for labor standards that have been drawn up in the interests of business, workers and their families. It is important to note that the law has meaning because it is enforced in an open system of government with checks and balances. Some countries have similar laws on the books but it is entirely up to the government as to whether the laws are enforced, and the people have no power or recourse to change things.

When Congress enacted the Occupational Safety and Health Act of 1970, the abbreviation "OSHA" became synonymous with meddlesome, counterproductive federal bureaucracy in the workplace. Stories traveled the nationwide grapevine about heavy-handed regulations and over-reaching federal inspectors.

OSHA became the lightning rod for opposing viewpoints about the costs and benefits of workplace regulation and the proper role of the government in this issue. Like all such regulations, those spawned by OSHA came at a price. So even as American business and industry haggled and argued and lobbied about workplace regulation they also began to comply with the law and add its costs to their products.

And once again, the emerging and evolving values of American society were codified in the form of laws and regulations that took root in our business and industry. Americans (the regulators and the regulated) rolled up their sleeves and went to work:

- To assure safe and healthful working conditions for working men and women;
- Encouraging the States in their efforts to assure safe and healthful working conditions; and
- Providing for research, information, education, and training in the field of occupational safety and health.

34

As it had with unfair wage and labor practices, the Congress found that personal injuries and illnesses arising out of work "impose a substantial burden upon, and are a hindrance to, interstate commerce in terms of lost production, wage loss, medical expense and disability compensation payments."

In other words, the intent was to provide protection and benefits to workers while making the whole system of production and commerce work more efficiently.

At Nucor we embrace these concepts and more. Safety of our employees is our number one priority and our wages are unequalled in our and many sectors of industry. Workers in our mills experience injury and illness at less than half the rate for U.S. manufacturing overall. In our steel mills our employees average more than $70,000 a year in salary.

In 2004, the U.S. Department of Labor reported that workplace fatalities had been reduced by more than 60 percent and occupational injury and illness by more than 40 percent since OSHA's inception — even as the workforce more than doubled.

OSHA continues to receive much scrutiny and debate. Regulators and business people and lawmakers continue to hammer away in that time-honored American pursuit of a practical, workable and fair system.

In the meantime, "Made in the USA" is stamped on products that reflect the values — and the costs — of our national commitment to workplace health and safety. In fiscal year 2005 taxpayers paid more than $468 million, almost half a billion dollars, just for the Occupational Safety and Health Administration. That is just the down payment on the total cost to our economy of compliance with occupational health and safety regulations.

But we as a people have agreed that this is something worth paying for. Furthermore, we have elevated occupational health and safety to a science. While many countries today do not require even basic workplace rules for worker safety and health, we in this country track millions of pieces of data and continually refine our models for improving safety, measuring results and determining financial costs and benefits. And today we see some of the best innovations coming from companies that are not motivated by the corrective hand of government but by their own desire to provide the safest, most productive workplace possible.

So, too, in the "outside world" — the world outside the plant. When it comes to protecting the environment American businesses long ago came to grips with environmental impacts that are measured in "parts per million" and "parts per billion." It's a pretty impressive fraction when the numerator is two places to the left of the decimal point and the denominator is nine places to the right. Yet for many industrial by-products these are the minuscule measures that we make.

Decades ago, American air had been seriously degraded by pollutants such as soot, smog, and smoke. We could see it with and feel it in our eyes. The air was dirty enough to burn your eyes and damage your lungs.

So once more, we rolled up our sleeves and got to work. Yet even as we have cleaned many pollutants from the sky, the air today is thick with the arguments and political agendas of global warming, acid rain, ozone holes high in the sky and ozone blankets down low to the ground, power plant emissions, gas-guzzling SUVs and more.

Once again we are sorting through the science, the pseudo-science and the political science. Politicians and polluters, tree-huggers and industrialists, gas hogs and hybrid vehicle pioneers.

The same era that gave rise to OSHA produced the Clean Air Act of 1970. The Congress had taken stock of the air in this country and found that the "predominant part" of our country's people lived in metropolitan and urban areas where the amount and "complexity" of air pollution had "resulted in mounting dangers to the public health and welfare, including injury to agricultural crops and livestock, damage to and the deterioration of property, and hazards to air and ground transportation."

The legislation's purposes included:
- Protect and enhance the quality of our air;
- Get the country moving forward with research and development to prevent and control air pollution;
- Provide technical and financial assistance for pollution control and prevention; and
- Promote regional air pollution prevention and control.

Although Nucor's steel recycling technology is many times cleaner and less polluting than the traditional integrated steel mills, the steel industry and other traditional "smokestack industries" have been at the center of the Clean Air Act. In the past 15 years the American steel industry has invested billions to make itself leaner and greener. Our

37

industry has reduced greenhouse gas emissions by more than 36 percent. In fact, we beat the greenhouse gas reduction goal set by the Kyoto Protocol by 600 percent.

But as with the federal legislation already mentioned, the Clean Air Act has been amended and has grown to embrace many aspects of America's life and economy beyond the old smokestack industries.

So this is who we are. This is what we stand for. A fair day's pay for a fair day's work. A workplace that does not compromise or threaten the health and safety of the workers. A way to make and transport goods at the least impact on the environment.

That's what "Made in America" stands for right?

If that is true, then what does "Bought in America" stand for? In 2005, the United States trade deficit for goods exceeded $781 billion, and the overall trade deficit was more than $725 billion — an all-time record that would have been considered unthinkable and unreachable just a few years ago. It has been great news for factories from Latin America to Asia. We are told that it is great news for the American consumer.

So what have we bought? Or more precisely, what have we bought into?

What we've bought is a bill of goods from foreign manufacturers and a global "free trade" framework that values cheap goods above the rule of law, workers rights, a clean environment, and the legitimate interests of our own citizens.

In one Chinese factory where athletic shoes are made, China Labor Watch, an independent watchdog organization, reported that Chinese workers endure "grueling hours, pitifully low wages, exploitation, abuse and denial of their rights."

In one example cited, factory workers labor from 7:30 a.m. to midnight, six to seven days a week, for wages of 31 cents an hour. They are crammed 12 to a room in dormitories and forced to eat food that barely sustains them. They have no real rights to organize and no effective channels to voice grievances or seek improved conditions.

China Labor Watch obtained pay stubs from another plant and determined that the average pay was equivalent to less than $55 a month, and about half of the workers' pay was docked for meals, dormitories and other fees. It was determined that both a husband and wife could not earn wages to meet the basic cost of living for the province in which the factory was located.

China's industrial regions, like the rest of the country, are largely powered by coal. In recent years, China's coal mining sector has come under harsh international scrutiny and criticism. China's mines kill 80 percent of the world's coal miners who die on the job. Official government death tolls exceed 6,000 miners per year, but many believe the actual toll to be much higher. The International Labor Office reports that more than 2.5 million Chinese labor in poorly-regulated or unregulated small-scale mines, which the ILO describes as "among the world's most dangerous."

What happens in China's coal mines should not be seen as separate from what goes on in its factories. It is part of the same production chain that competes with manufactured goods from the United States and elsewhere.

The Wall Street Journal has reported that the Chinese government censors press coverage of mining disasters and that implementation of mine safety laws is "sporadic at best." Many of China's mining disasters involve hundreds of miners and many occur at mines that are owned by the state itself.

China's industrial system preys particularly hard on more than 150 million rural, surplus workers, many of whom are forced to move from one job to the next to provide for basic subsistence. China's government continues a high-stakes balancing act of development and exploitation across every sector of its economy. Its people are the "cannon fodder" in a well-orchestrated, long-range economic campaign by their country's dictatorial government.

Human rights groups have reported the violation of basic workers' rights of those who protest government abuses and worker exploitation. Protestors and organizers face punishment ranging from extended prison terms to possible death sentences. Those who are imprisoned face beatings, torture and unbearable conditions.

The government values totalitarian control and order above basic human rights. It also values production and lower costs above environmental stewardship. The World Bank reported that by the late 1990s Chinese industry accounted for more than 70 percent of the nation's total pollution — no small feat in a nation of 1.3 billion people.

China essentially has provided its industrial base with a huge subsidy by permitting it to expand its capacity without incurring costs of pollution control. The central government in effect pushed responsibility for pollution abatement to the provincial and local level where enforcement has proved uneven at best and corrupt and ineffective at worst.

A cornerstone of pollution enforcement in China is the pollution levy, in which fees are charged based on the discharge of pollutants above limits set by the state. A World Bank study reported that much of the burden for enforcement of these levies falls on municipal governments with limited enforcement resources. "As a result," the World Bank reported, "many polluters can effectively avoid paying charges, fines or other penalties."

Often the polluters and the local agencies negotiate how much of the levy will ultimately be paid. The study reported that firms from the private sector "appear to have" less bargaining power than state-owned enterprises, and that firms facing adverse financial situations are more likely to pay less pollution levies than enforcement would otherwise require.

Like China's air, China's government and its pollution enforcement system lacks transparency, and it is often difficult to shine the light of day through it. What is known is that the national government continues to promote the widespread use of coal to fuel industrial expansion and continues to allow old, outdated, heavily polluting plants and factories to operate on a massive scale.

The result, according to the World Bank, is that air pollution "exceeded World Health Organization safety standards by very large margins," and "hundreds of thousands of people are dying or becoming seriously ill from pollution-related respiratory disease." The agency also reported that in the decade 1987 to 1997, even as Chinese industry expanded at double-digit rates, "regulatory incentives for air pollution control have actually weakened. . . [and] regulatory enforcement has apparently weakened."

Acid rain falls on more than 30 percent of China's land, and China is the second-largest emitter of the greenhouse gas carbon dioxide.

The World Bank reported that many of China's waterways are "close to biological death" from excessive discharges of industrial pollutants, which make the waters unfit for direct human use.

The World Health Organization reported that seven of the world's ten most polluted cities are Chinese cities. The U.S. National Aeronautic and Space Administration has tracked massive clouds of air pollution and described the "considerable outflow of pollution from China and southeast Asia." The agency has described an "Asian plume" that "can be followed as it propagates over the Pacific Ocean and in some instances this plume reaches the west coast of the United States." Satellite images of this massive pollution can be found on the Internet.

In the summer of 2002 something called the "Asian Brown Cloud" made headlines in the U.S. The news reports summarized the science and politics of a growing cloud of pollution over India and South Asia as well as the cloud that was growing over China and East Asia. Scientific arguments about the causes and impacts of the cloud were reported in newspapers, broadcasts and in Internet news outlets.

The political hot air generated by these debates added to global warming as politicians in Asia found their countries accused of contributing to global warming as much as the United States. Asian politicians complained to the United Nations that the term "Asian Brown Cloud" reflected poorly on their countries so the U.N. did the politically correct thing: By a stroke of the pen the "Asian Brown Cloud" conveniently became the "Atmospheric Brown Cloud." They didn't even have to change the "ABC" acronym in their paperwork.

But the name doesn't eliminate the many causes of the huge pollution cloud, including the fact that millions of poor Asians must meet subsistence needs by cooking and heating with open fires. When hundreds of millions of people live in poverty their individual actions can add up to big environmental impacts.

But Asia's brown clouds also result from industrial development such as that in China, where growing financial resources are funneled away from pollution control to other purposes.

Meanwhile, the U.S. economy is being pressured by domestic and international politics to further increase efficiency, reduce emissions and even curtail economic growth to address global warming. Statistically, while the Chinese have used tactics such as illegal currency manipulation to move manufacturing out of the United States and into China, air pollutants are in excess of 650 times higher in China than comparable U.S. operations.

And the final irony and insult can be found in the fact that China is also exporting its pollution to our country, whether you choose to call it the "Asian Brown Cloud" or a Brown Cloud by another name. China is among the largest sources of mercury pollution in the U.S., and up to 25 percent of the particulate pollution over California can come from across the Pacific.

There is a conventional phrase in use these days: "poverty as a weapon." This term usually describes how regimes in developing countries work to keep wages so low that developed countries cannot compete with them in manufacturing that requires unskilled labor. Textiles and apparel manufacturing are good examples.

When you look at the example of Communist China you see this concept describing the full arsenal of this country's totalitarian system. The lack of meaningful wage and hour protections enables Chinese companies and multinationals to exploit a huge workforce on a massive scale.

The lack of basic political freedoms and the rule of law permits the state's gulags and its political prisoners to provide forced labor for the industrial sector. This form of political poverty not only exploits the prisoners directly, it enables the state to make examples of them in oppressing workers throughout China.

With regard to its environmental practices China takes advantage of its status as a developing nation to shift responsibility for environmental clean-up onto the backs of developed nations such as the United States and European nations.

In 2005, Americans were jarred from their indifference to China when it was announced that the state-owned Chinese oil giant was maneuvering to purchase California-based Unocal. Another state-owned enterprise made a bid on U.S. appliance maker Maytag. Many Americans unconcerned about the massive flow of U.S. wealth to China became concerned when they realized the Chinese had at their disposal hundreds of billions of dollars to start buying up America's energy and industrial assets.

So here is a country that is not investing in closing or cleaning up power plants and factories but is embarked on a concerted effort to buy up energy reserves, world-class American brands, and American manufacturing capability. In every sense of the word it has used poverty as a weapon — including financial poverty, political poverty and environmental poverty.

The money not paid its exploited workers, the money not invested in the environment, the money harvested from its prisoners has all been used by a totalitarian regime to undercut and undermine American manufacturers. Now they are poised to repatriate the money we freely spent in order to purchase our own energy and industrial assets.

China's apologists will tell us that it has laws on the books to provide for minimum wages and to protect employee health and safety. They will point to environmental laws and various examples of environmental progress. They will point out to us that we buy Chinese-made goods willingly because it saves us money.

But the facts remain that the means of production, the press, the Internet and all communications media, the political apparatus, the law of the land, and the actions of 1.3 billion people all remain under the top-down control of a highly-centralized, totalitarian, one-party state. When we confront that level of control, and a well-honed national strategy to seize every advantage in the marketplace, we must be willing to engage in some tough diplomacy and hard-hitting competition.

Earlier in this chapter I sketched three laws that have had a profound effect on the way that we manufacture goods — the Fair Wage and Labor Act, the Occupational Safety and Health Act, and the Clean Air Act.

We can find similar words in "laws" that have been written in China and other totalitarian states. What gives laws their meaning is not how they look on paper. For a law to be legitimate it must be enforced fairly and openly. Its provisions and enforcement should be open to the scrutiny of the people, through a free press and the democratic process. No one branch of government should be given arbitrary power to change the law or to choose whether it will be enforced.

So how does an open, democratic society with legitimate laws compete on a level playing field with a totalitarian state such as China?

Here's where the alphabet soup of modern international trade comes into play. Every high school student in American should receive some basic schooling in the NAFTAs, CAFTAs, GATTs, WTOs, and all the trade agreements, treaties and organizations that regulate international trade. These should be introduced into every civics curriculum at the high school level. We are seeing a significant shift of power and political effort toward them, and our ability to deal with them effectively will determine whether we maintain our manufacturing base and our economic strength.

The emergence of these global and international trade frameworks is a defining political event of this era. They are not only revolutionizing world trade, they force us to wrestle with fundamental questions:

- Do we put the interests of the American people ahead of our obligations under international trade agreements and treaties?
- If we perceive that other nations are not playing by the rules and we judge that the rules are not being enforced do we go our own way or remain engaged?
- Do we continue to promote "free trade" in an arena where many trading partners are clearly engaged in "managed trade?"
- Do we remain committed to enforcing the provisions of "free trade" even when we don't see "fair trade?"

These international agreements and treaties directly tie our fortunes and our fate to nations that are vastly different from ours in terms of their values, their systems of government and the way that they conduct trade. China serves as the biggest, most important example. Both China and the U.S. are members of the World Trade Organization, or WTO. If the WTO is effective and fair, things will go better. If it is ineffective or unfair then we've got problems.

The WTO is just over a decade old, having been established in January 1995 from nine years of negotiations in what was called the "Uruguay Round." Nearly 150 countries are members, and they account for the bulk of the world's trade. The WTO was established to provide a forum for trade negotiations and to administer trade agreements. It also handles trade disputes and monitors national trade policies.

By its own description the WTO works to adopt agreements through consensus as opposed to one-nation-one-vote. By its own admission this means that the WTO often takes a very long time to arrive at decisions, and once it does, the wording may be so vague and ambiguous that it is hard to interpret, much less enforce its agreements.

Forging trade agreements and settling disputes doesn't grab many headlines. Yet the little-noticed decisions of the WTO have enormous impacts on our industry and our people. I hope as time goes by we can find ways to raise the profile of these issues and grab the attention of more Americans.

But let's face facts: If the United States disapproves of Japan's liquor taxes, Mexico's antidumping duties on corn syrup, or India's lack of patent protections, how do we command the interest and concern of average citizens?

The simple truth is that to have free trade, all countries must abide by the international rules which ensure open markets. This basic principal points us toward rigorous enforcement and awareness.

WTO decisions and dispute settlements directly affect significant sectors of our economy and how we conduct business. Steel provides an important recent example. In March 2002, President Bush placed tariffs on imported steel to address a broader range of issues and countries in the same vein as the countervailing duties against steel from Brazil, Japan and Russia I mentioned earlier.

President Bush's decision took political courage in this free trade era when "tariffs" is almost a dirty word. He recognized that companies with about half of the country's steel production capacity were facing potential bankruptcy. At the same time the U.S. steel industry was putting forth a tremendous effort to consolidate, boost its productivity and better deal with the onslaught of steel in the global market. The protections afforded by the tariffs were intended to stem the tide of steel imports so that U.S. steelmakers could complete their competitive overhaul. His decision was both prudent and far-sighted.

But U.S. trading partners protested and took their case to the WTO, which ruled that the tariffs were a barrier to free trade and a violation of trade agreements. As a result, President Bush lifted the tariffs at the end of 2003, more than a year ahead of schedule.

So who "won" and who "lost"? Did the U.S. "back down" instead of confronting the WTO? Was this issue worth ratcheting up a diplomatic or public relations war? We as Americans are just starting to feel our way through such questions as we navigate a new world of international trade and diplomacy. The fact is that all member nations of the WTO are engaged in a massive experiment: How to manage the trade-off of lost national sovereignty and power versus potential gains from more international trade.

From 2003 through 2005 the world watched a David-and-Goliath contest at the WTO. One of the world's smallest nations, Antigua and Barbuda, with a population of about 70,000, took on the United States in the WTO, claiming that

49

the U.S. ban on Internet gambling was an illegal infringement on Antigua Barbuda's online enterprises.

The United States position was based on several states' laws banning such gambling, so the question of sovereignty extended all the way to that level of government. But the states' laws and the U.S. national position did not carry the day at the WTO, which ruled that U.S. laws against Internet gambling violated WTO rules — and imposed a deadline for the U.S. to comply with the ruling.

Since its beginning as a nation the United States has focused on the right way to engage in trade in order to increase prosperity and enhance security. America's situation today has been many decades in the making. It's a history that transcends party lines and has its roots in The Great Depression, the devastation of World War II and the Cold War.

For several decades in the 1800s the collection of tariffs by the U.S. federal government provided a significant portion of federal revenues. Tariffs were basically imposed as a tax on trade to fund the government. When more revenues were needed, to fund the Civil War for instance, the federal government would raise tariffs. During the 19th century tariff revenues as a percent of imports spiked as high as 45 percent and plunged as low as under 10 percent.

The miraculous invention of the income tax pushed tariffs into the background, and the tariff percentage of merchandise imports declined until The Great Depression. But when the Depression first tightened its grip on our country the U.S. Congress passed the Smoot-Hawley Tariff Act of 1930. In the decades since, "Smoot Hawley" has become synonymous with "protectionism" and an example of the kind of legislation that can precipitate trade wars.

Some historians brand Smoot-Hawley as a primary culprit in pushing the Depression into The Great Depression. The legislation's high tariffs were originally designed to protect American farmers from a flood of imports resulting from massive European overproduction. But when America's trading partners retaliated with protectionist measures of their own, overall trade declined dramatically. U.S. exports to Europe declined from more than $2.3 billion in 1929 to $784 million in 1932. Imports from Europe plummeted from more than $1.3 billion to just $390 million during that period. The debate continues today as to whether the collapse of international trade should be blamed on Smoot-Hawley or on the stock market crash and onset of The Great Depression.

Today, more than 75 years after its enactment, "Smoot Hawley" is routinely used as a Bronx cheer by free trade advocates. But in balancing arguments for and against free trade there are many intermediate positions between pure free trade and the branding iron of Smoot Hawley. There are really many models of free trade and managed trade.

Nevertheless, those who call for any kind of legitimate trade protections can be unfairly branded with this famous piece of legislation. Larry Kudlow, host of Kudlow & Company on CNBC, labeled Sen. Charles Schumer (Democrat of New York) and Sen. Lindsay Graham (Republican of South Carolina) as "senators Smoot Schumer and Hawley Graham." They earned these nicknames when they introduced legislation that proposed a countervailing tariff on Chinese imports unless the Chinese government ended its deliberate manipulation of currency exchange rates to give Chinese manufacturers an unfair advantage.

Smoot-Hawley actually followed other legislation enacted during the 1920s that also imposed or raised tariffs. Just as today's political tide runs strongly in favor of free trade, the trend in that era was to protect American farmers and industry. At the time, tariffs appeared to have worked.

An interesting sidelight to Smoot-Hawley is that during the debate over the issue President Hoover pushed for a Tariff Commission that could act swiftly to adjust tariffs by up to 50 percent. It reminds me of the "fast track" authority that recent trade legislation has given the U.S president for negotiating trade agreements. From Smoot-Hawley right through today we are always trying to equip governments to keep up with markets — and with other governments.

More American students should be taught about Smoot-Hawley — not whether it was all bad or half bad or half good, but rather how it has shaped our economic history and continues to influence our perceptions of trade, protectionism and foreign policy.

Just five years after Smoot-Hawley, in 1934, the Reciprocal Trade Agreement Act authorized the president to negotiate bi-lateral trade agreements, paving the way for the U.S. to sit down with trading partners one at a time and try to hammer out lower tariffs and trade barriers and in general put their mutual trade on sounder footing.

The legislation is viewed as a reaction to Smoot-Hawley and also is credited with establishing a pattern for trade negotiations that has grown and evolved into our present system. It also refined the concept of "Most Favored Nation," which was a lynchpin of modern trade negotiations for decades.

Just as The Great Depression traumatized Western economic systems, World War II delivered a stunning blow to nations' assumptions about how the world was supposed to work. From the rubble of that war the nations of the world cobbled together the United Nations and other political frameworks that constituted a fresh approach to trade, among other issues.

People who follow the news carefully may recognize the term GATT, which stands for General Agreement on Tariffs and Trade. As the charter for post-war international trade it also became the first-draft blueprint for international trade as we know it today. When historians write books about 21st century trade and politics they will trace many of these events back to 1947 and GATT.

GATT was not like the United Nations, with its name on a building. It was basically an agreement that grew and evolved as an international framework for what were called "Rounds." These were essentially long, drawn-out negotiations, and during the '40s, '50s and '60s they focused primarily on reducing tariffs. It was a busy time. The world was trying to rebuild from the World War, and it was divided and polarized by the Cold War. At the same time the industrialized nations were trying to hammer out ways to reduce tariffs.

During the 1970s, the GATT Tokyo Round focused on "non-tariff barriers." This generic-sounding category included a range of actions that provide the home country's industries or products with a built-in advantage. This has the same effect as raising a barrier to competitors from outside the country.

A prime example is government subsidy, which gives the home-grown producers a cost and price advantage in the marketplace. Another example is to create bureaucratic roadblocks that make it difficult or expensive for other countries' products to enter your own markets. Complex, obstructive procurement regulations have been used to weed out and discourage foreign competition. Product standards can be rigged to discriminate effectively against foreign products. Trade negotiators spent a lot of time during the Tokyo Round trying to deal with non-tariff barriers.

The U.S. government also focused on non-tariff barriers in the 1970s and passed the Trade Act of 1974 to authorize the President to negotiate with other nations on these issues. This was an important milestone in the evolution of trade policy because Congress specifically linked trade to a wider slate of government policies and actions — not just tariffs.

The Jackson-Vanik amendment to this act specifically linked trade policy to human rights and also widened the circle of stakeholders to include human rights activists and others that could now link trade policy to these wider concerns.   Today's focus on human rights, environmental policies and other issues in the context of trade agreements can be linked to this landmark 1974 legislation. A decade later the definition of unfair trading practices would be expanded in The Trade and Tariff Act of 1984.

In the 1980s the U.S. and other countries were still managing a great number of trade-related issues on a piecemeal basis. For example the steel industry in the 1970s faced rapidly rising steel imports, including significant amounts that were dumped into the market at prices below cost. A so-called "trigger price mechanism" was implemented that allowed the government to establish minimum prices for imported steel, in an effort to counteract the dumping.

Shortly after that, in 1985, the U.S., France, West Germany, United Kingdom and Japan negotiated the Plaza Accord, which established a program to systematically devalue the U.S. dollar relative to the yen and the Deutsche mark — with the stated aim of restoring balance to our country's massive trade deficit. At that time the issue of currency imbalance was deemed important enough to convene the world's leading economic powers to deal with it.

By the 1980s, GATT had embarked on the Uruguay Round. These negotiations gave rise to the WTO and largely shaped the international trade arena as we know it today. The Uruguay Round lasted from 1986 through 1994, during the administrations of Presidents Reagan, Bush and Clinton. The Berlin Wall came down during those years, and other events had their share of headlines, but just as with other landmark trade events, "The Uruguay Round" largely escaped the notice of us average Americans.

But during that same time another trade negotiation made its share of headlines. The North American Free Trade Agreement, or NAFTA, became a household word and a big issue in the presidential election of 1992. Third party candidate Ross Perot famously coined the expression "that giant sucking sound" in predicting and describing the loss of American jobs to Mexico as a result of NAFTA.

The Congress ratified NAFTA in 1993, setting in motion the gradual elimination of all tariff barriers among Canada, the U.S., and Mexico. NAFTA built upon an earlier free trade agreement between the U.S. and Canada, which had already integrated their two economies to a high degree.

NAFTA also reduced non-tariff barriers, including various regulatory restrictions, import quotas and licensing requirements. Mexico had to liberalize restrictions on foreign ownership of industries and open its banking sector.

NAFTA's true believers projected hundreds of thousands of new American jobs. President Clinton predicted that two years after it went into effect 200,000 American jobs would be created. NAFTA's opponents predicted job losses in the millions.

The Congressional Research Office in 2003 updated a report on some of NAFTA's effects on industry for the period 1993 to 2001. The report said that the overall effect was "relatively small, primarily because two-way trade with Mexico amounts to less than three percent of U.S. GDP (gross domestic product)."

But NAFTA offers examples of how specific and important changes are set in motion when nations are competing in an environment where the rules are changed.

Textile and apparel imports from Mexico during that period increased significantly (386 percent), and computer equipment imports soared upward by 397 percent. Automotive industry trade increased the most in dollar terms, in both exports (up $21.8 billion) and imports ($49.6 billion). The U.S. microelectronics industry saw the greatest percentage increase in exports, up 268 percent.

NAFTA eliminated U.S. tariffs and quotas and Mexican tariffs on textiles and apparel goods manufactured in and sold between the two countries. Total trade in these goods increased 250 percent while the U.S. trade deficit in these goods jumped 455 percent.

Competing studies and statistics don't always agree on how much damage this creates to U.S. manufacturers. Some claim that it is better for manufacturing jobs to go to Mexico or other countries in the Americas than to Asia because this will preserve more business for U.S. suppliers. This argument has been used in recent years to promote CAFTA, the 2005 free trade agreement for our hemisphere involving the U.S. and several Central American neighbors.

The Congressional Research Office study reported that Mexico's share of U.S. motor vehicle trade increased from 5 percent to 17 percent during the period and that some of Mexico's vehicle exports to the U.S. were displacing those from other countries. Motor vehicle imports from Mexico increased by a hefty 475 percent.

The impact on America's manufacturing sector and American jobs overall is debated, and competing statistics are used by opposing camps. The Congressional Research Office report used two statistics to bracket the potential job losses from NAFTA. It cited the Economic Policy Institute's (EPI) estimate that 766,000 existing or potential jobs were lost due to NAFTA. EPI also reported that the NAFTA Transitional Adjustment Assistant Program had certified 330,062 workers affected. The actual number of job losses, the report said, "may lie in a range between the number of NAFTA-TAA certifications and the EPI figure."

57

Still, it's a lot of jobs — and it's just one trade agreement.

Two aspects of these free trade agreements interest me. First, they have become the lightning rod for trade issues in general, even though they are just one part of the picture. Second, they seem to redefine the boundaries and the definition of "us." With NAFTA for instance, the "us" is no longer the U.S., it is Canada, the U.S. and Mexico. We created a trade framework in which "we" are defined as the three countries of North America, and we talk about how to create advantages for manufacturers, farmers and others in those three countries.

In 2005 Mexican steel companies and the Mexican steel industry became increasingly concerned that such nations India, Russia, Turkey, and China were engaged in unfair trade practices to sell steel products at artificially low prices within the North American market. They set in motion a process for the governments and steel industries in Canada, the U.S. and Mexico to deliver a report to the North American Steel Trade Committee to deal with this issue and other priorities.

The three nations were also preparing a coordinated presentation and discussion of steel issues before the World Trade Organization.

This is not only an outgrowth of NAFTA but of the North American Security and Prosperity Initiative, in which the three North American nations cooperate on trade-related issues, product standards, regulations and security issues, including those related to the flow of people and goods across their borders.

When the U.S. Congress voted on the Central America Free Trade Agreement (CAFTA) in 2005, the 1990s enthusiasm for free trade agreements had been tempered with a skepticism that resulted from the weak U.S. trade posture and disastrous trade deficits. With only a two-vote margin in the U.S. House of Representatives the media managed to find room among the baseball steroid stories, Supreme Court nominees and other headlines for some talk about trade.

CAFTA opponents looked at the hundreds of thousands of lost jobs and started asking some tough questions. Why shouldn't we make stronger links between better labor and environmental protections and free trade? Why shouldn't we consider the long-term consequences of gutting major sectors of U.S. manufacturing?

But these regional free trade frameworks are probably here to stay because they can serve a variety of economic and political purposes. For example, the Central European Free Trade Agreement has grown to include eight nations that were formerly part of the Soviet Bloc. A key purpose in establishing this free trade agreement was for these countries to establish a pathway for joining the European Union.

SAFTA stands for South Asia Free Trade Agreement, which is leading to the creation of a free trade zone covering almost 1.5 billion people across South Asia, including India. Ultimately these countries will virtually eliminate tariffs in trading with each other. It is a safe bet that such trade arrangements not only shape the economics of the group but also in the long term re-shape their political identity as a member of the group.

"Politics makes strange bedfellows," goes the old saying. So does trade. I began this chapter by looking at some milestones in U.S. history that define our progress and evolution as a society. It is a remarkable history in which we took our industrial might and transformed it into labor laws and environmental laws that define the progressive compact that we have forged between industry and our society as a whole. We built our values into what we make.

In today's world our nation and others are moving through a rapidly shifting maze of political and economic alliances. New global organizations such as the WTO have important impacts on our domestic industries and our workers. Regional free trade agreements are redefining our very sense of who "we" are.

Some of our most important trading relationships are not with countries with which we have the closest political ties. Many important trading relationships are with nations whose governments do not recognize or respect the human rights that are fundamental to our society. Many people tell us to accept these differences in the name of "pluralism" or other vague terms. Many people tell us that through increased trade ties we can promote greater freedom and openness in the societies of our trading partners.

And this is all well and good. But when we trade we should never trade away our self-reliance in manufacturing, our national security, or our commitment to continue the social and economic progress that we have worked so hard to bring to our people.

That progress has been built on manufacturing.

CHAPTER 3
WORST CASE SCENARIO

From 1998 to 2005 the United States lost more than 3.3 million manufacturing jobs. Many of those jobs have moved to countries where basic human rights are not recognized or protected and where environmental protection is systematically ignored on a massive scale. We have transferred an enormous amount of our productive capacity to nations that are actively using human rights abuses and environmental degradation to achieve an economic advantage over us.

When Congress passed the Trade Act of 2002 it included provisions that the U.S. government make an accounting of labor rights in countries with which we're negotiating trade agreements. These "core labor standards" include:

- A prohibition on the use of any form of forced or compulsory labor;
- A minimum age for the employment of children; and
- Acceptable conditions of work with respect to minimum wages, hours of work and occupational safety and health.

If we are negotiating free trade agreements with a nation then the U.S. government is required to submit a labor rights report on that country to the Congress so that these fundamental rights can be considered during trade negotiations. The government tracks workers' rights for broader diplomatic purposes as well.

Here are two statistics I would like to track: During an average year of shopping, how many labels does the average

American shopper read that are printed with "Made in China" or "Made in Vietnam?" The number for the China label would be huge. The number for the Vietnam label would be much, much smaller, but growing steadily.

Along with those statistics I'd like to track, "How many news stories did you read this year about human rights violations in China or Vietnam?" Again, I am not picking on the media. The content of the news says more about us than it does about the media.

As a former adversary turned trading partner Vietnam certainly stands apart. It will forever be the landmark of where the Cold War got hot and stayed hot for years. The nation remains a Communist dictatorship, with one-party rule that controls every aspect of everyday life, stifles basic freedoms and commands the national economy.

In 2001 the U.S.-Vietnam Bilateral Trade Agreement went into effect with predictable results: In just two years Vietnam's exports to our country grew more than four-fold, to more than $4.5 billion in 2003. Manufactured goods dominated, and apparel was chief among them. American consumers are most likely to wear their "Made in Vietnam" labels.

In testimony before the U.S. Congress, Human Rights Watch called attention to the following human rights violations:

- Hundreds of religious and political prisoners remain behind bars. Vietnam's prisons are characterized by cramped, dark, unsanitary cells, and prisoners can be subjected to beating, kicking and electric shock batons.

- Prison terms as long as 20 years have been imposed on religious minorities and members of churches not approved by the Communist regime. Members of Christian and Buddhist denominations are beaten, detained and forced to recant their faith.
- Dissidents have been jailed for the "crimes" of calling for democratic reforms or using the Internet to spread the word about human rights and religious freedom.
- No independent media exist in the country. The entire apparatus is state-controlled, and direct criticism of the Communist Party is forbidden.

That's Human Rights with the "Made in Vietnam" label. A report on worker rights prepared by the U.S. Department of Labor said point-blank, "There is no true freedom of association in Vietnam." The country's laws do provide for collective bargaining, ban the exploiting of children and limits their work hours to 7 hours a day or 42 hours per week. The extent of child labor was not clear, but the International Labor Organization reported that during 1998 more than 995,000 children were "economically active" in the country. Many of these work on farms or in the informal sector, and the report states that the "percentage of child labor found in the manufacturing industry is negligible. . . ."

While it is easy enough to speak of the Iron Curtain in the past tense, the Bamboo Curtain still makes it difficult to comprehend fully the lack of human rights in Vietnam.

China is a somewhat different story. As this nation has emerged as an economic giant it has discovered that it belongs in the international spotlight. With its economic growth and power come the unwanted attentions of human rights activists, labor organizers, and overseas competitors.

As Vietnam illustrates, there is always the ethical and moral consideration of trading with a country that does not respect and preserve basic human rights. Traders, multinationals and everyday consumers must ask themselves if they want to do business with such governments and systems.

But there comes into play an additional question, and China serves as a good focus for such a question. It might be phrased something like this: "Does the totalitarian Communist state of [China] systematically exploit human rights violations, environmental depredations, trade law violations, and the economic disadvantage of its own people to accomplish military-industrial-political advantage in the global arena?"

See the difference? Do you cut such countries a break because they are "struggling to emerge from Socialism?" Do you chalk up abuses of worker rights to a society that's "in transition?" Do you excuse the manipulation of currency because the country's banking system has not "fully evolved?" Or do all of these add up to something more?

As big as China has become in global trade it is still very difficult for outsiders to know precisely what goes on in its government and industry. Just as with its Communist little brother Vietnam, China does not permit an independent media or political opposition to challenge the status quo. So what does the status quo look like inside China?

China Labor Watch has brought important examples of how China's manufacturing juggernaut depends at least in part on what can only be called the exploitation of workers.

Consider China Labor Watch's report of a footwear factory where workers were on the job for up to 81 hours per week, and where overtime pay was actually less than regular pay. Workers were threatened with physical abuse, termination and subject to harassment for any complaints.

At a toy factory workers were kept in the factory for 16 ½ hours a day and worked 12 ½ of those hours. Average wage equated to 13 cents per hour. Workers had to work 120 consecutive days before getting one day off and had to work 70 days before getting the full pay for their first month. Seventeen workers lived in one dormitory room and two people must share a lower berth.

Accountability for such conditions is hard to pin down in this "multilateral" age in which we live. The footwear factory, for instance, was financed from Taiwan. The toy factory's products are given away with American fast food meals. There is nothing stamped on these products to tell the consumer about how the products are made and who is accountable. The only clue may be the words "Made in China."

One label you will not see on any products is "Made in Laogai." It would be a worthwhile human rights/consumer initiative to require goods made in Laogai to be so labeled. Where is Laogai? It is anywhere in China that forced labor is used to produce and manufacture goods. The word means "reform through labor" and it has been used as a slogan by the Chinese Communists to describe their system of prison labor.

As with most things in China there are no precise, independent accountings for the number of people in Chinese prisons who are forced to work in manufacturing, and likewise no firm estimate of how many products made by forced prison labor find their way into U.S. markets.

The Laogai Research Foundation describes it as "the largest system of forced labor prisons in the world." It goes on to report, "These camps house both criminal and political offenders together and all are forced to labor." And it is this point of course that separates Laogai from run-of-the-mill prison labor. Prisoners who are paying a debt to society for crimes can reasonably be expected to work and pay back society. Prisoners who themselves are victims of human rights violations are an entirely different matter.

The foundation also reports that the Laogai system of prison camps, modeled on the Soviet Gulag, "have become prosperous machines to generate revenue. Laogai products continue to find their way into the international market, despite the attempts of bilateral agreements between the U.S. and China to stop their exportation."

That is a polite way of reporting that the Chinese government is committed to maintaining control through political repression, but is not committed to the rule of law. It is also a particularly offensive example of how the government exploits its own citizens for financial and economic advantage.

These atrocities, and many more, point to the absolute hypocrisy of those who suggest that we should not seek to enforce our international agreements — as against free trade. Free trade? Trade being financed through illegal currency manipulation, human rights abuses and utter disregard for environmental protection is not free at all. It might better be described as a free-for-all in international trade.

Amnesty International reported that an offshoot of the Laogai, China's "Re-education through Labor" system, the Laojiao, is to be reformed by the government, but that "the exact nature and scope of reform remain unclear." The Re-education through Labor system detains thousands of people a year, according to Amnesty International, and the system's victims are detained for up to four years without being charged or given a trial.

According to the Amnesty International Report 2005, "Tens of thousands of people continued to be detained or imprisoned in violation of their fundamental human rights and were at high risk of torture or ill-treatment. Thousands of people were sentenced to death or executed, many after unfair trials."

The human rights watchdog also reported, "The rights of freedom of expression and association of workers' representatives continued to be severely curtailed and independent trade unions remain illegal."

Chinese citizens can be detained or imprisoned just for accessing or circulating information on the Internet that the totalitarian state finds threatening.

Americans were justifiably upset when U.S. Internet giant Google announced that it would collaborate with the Chinese Communist government in restricting the access of Chinese citizens to online information. In responding to the outcry by freedom-loving Americans and international human rights groups, Google cleverly positioned its decision as a matter of "quality."

The company cited that its lack of a local presence in China resulted in the system being down about 10 percent of the time, occasional slowness in the system and search results that could browser."

So the Chinese get faster browsing, but their march toward freedom is stalled by their own government and willing U.S. commercial collaborators.

At the very least we should be wary of "trading partners" that do not value truth and the free flow of information. Free trade must be built on trust. How do we deal with trading partners that systematically suppress the truth? And are collaboration and kow-towing the best way to influence a still totalitarian regime?

But a more specific question remains? How should Chinese human rights abuses and violations influence our trade policy? Are competing economic systems still squared off in a high-stakes contest? It seemed clear to us during the Cold War that we needed to contain or combat the spread of totalitarian Communist states. Today it seems like the "free trade" ideology is in the driver's seat of our foreign policy and that our commitment to free trade sometimes trumps our commitment to free people. But is it really free? No. What we are confronting today is a distorted form of free trade and not true free trade at all.

China's economy is often described with terms like "hybrid" or phrases like "one foot in the Communist past and one foot in the capitalist future." I'll bet it doesn't look like a "hybrid" to workers who are forced to live and work in poverty and squalor. Such polite terms may ring hollow with political prisoners who are forced to labor and who face unjust imprisonment or execution.

The fact is this: China is still a Communist state, and it uses all of the traditional tools of that system to preserve its power and to achieve economic advantage. What has changed since the Cold War is that we no longer challenge or confront this system in the traditional ways. We are instead transferring our productive capacity and our wealth into a Communist state at a record pace.

We are freely giving away what we should normally fight to protect. The war — not the battle — is being lost without a shot fired. Shame on us!

As a steel company executive I have watched with growing concern over the past several years as our nation has lost its political focus on some fundamental issues regarding freedom, fair trade and the need to nurture a healthy manufacturing sector. The examples I have cited for China are just a few examples from one country. We can find other examples from different countries where our foreign policy seems driven by the blind faith in expanding trade while turning a blind eye to the damage we are doing to our own people and our own industries.

China illustrates how a totalitarian regime can gear up its entire system to achieve an advantage over its competitors. And the crucial point of this is not that China's currency manipulation, oppressed workforce, dangerous mines, and pollution-belching industries equip it to undersell the competition. The crucial point is that all of these forces are sapping the U.S. economy of our fundamental capability to produce.

There seems to be more than just a few business executives and their politicians who want to stand behind these practices, taking a blind eye toward the negative realities, in the name of short-term gains and "free trade."

Our current distorted version of free trade may play into the short-term interests of certain businesses, providing them with low-cost materials or opportunities for offshoring that are too good to pass up. They find themselves in a position to espouse a free trade of convenience, allowing them to chant the mantra of free trade while taking advantage of what will prove to be short-term gains.

Is this really free trade? Where one side plays by the rules and the other openly flaunts illegal practices — absolutely not. Free trade is a system of open markets guided by rules which prohibit patently illegal acts such as manipulating currencies in order to gain a grossly unfair advantage.

For that reason, American manufacturers have been compelled to get involved and to start pushing for change in U.S. foreign policy and trade policy. The wealth of this country has been built on industrial leadership, innovation and production. It is not a stretch to declare that we have preserved and advanced liberty here and around the world through our industrial strength. In every war we have fought and won for freedom, our industrial might has earned a share of the credit.

Does unbridled and illegal free trade at any price advance the cause of freedom? Ask the political prisoners in the Laogai. Ask the Americans in factory towns and mill towns whose jobs, old-age security and way of life are gone forever. Free trade as a principle is good. **Free trade as an ideology, without enforcement of well-reasoned rules, takes away our resolve to preserve our own industrial and manufacturing base**.

We call them "trading partners" and this has a friendly ring to it. It makes us think of dancing partners or business partners. The term therefore can mislead us when we talk about trade. My intentions are not to limit reasoned and enforceable free trade, nor is it to slow the development of developing nations, but I also do not intend to sit idly by while governments pillage the communities of American workers through dishonest, deceitful and patently illegal acts — especially while they preside over the systematic oppression of their own citizens.

The peculiar thing about international trade is that it contains all of these elements. As "trading partners" we are joined together in a kind of dance. But we're also business partners. We are joined through common enterprises and businesses in which both sides seek rewards and benefits. And yes, we are sometimes rivals, if not adversaries.

Sometimes in trade and politics push does come to shove. When it does are we willing to put our national interests ahead of other considerations? Nucor Steel and other manufacturers have reached the point of answering "Yes." After all, we are competitors as well. That is why we are working to forge a new political consensus that focuses on true, undistorted free trade and that can create and strengthen comprehensive pro-manufacturing policies here in the U.S.

In the Cold War we brought together every military, economic and political tool at our disposal to contain the spread of political repression and totalitarianism. In today's trade arena we issue statements at meetings, we dispatch trade representatives to make speeches and we ask everyone involved to please exercise "patience" as we work through these issues.

Patience would be a virtue indeed if everything would just stop moving while we attend meetings and negotiations that drag out over years. Recalling the Chinese strategy of currency manipulation that I mentioned in Chapter 1 it is worth restating here that China first pegged its currency to the dollar in 1994. **For more than 13 years the country has carefully maintained its clear-eyed strategy to artificially devalue its currency over time. When you are cheating, time is on your side until you are made to stop cheating**. Given the pace of change and the magnitude of change in today's global markets, China's currency regime has had a very long lifespan indeed.

The impacts of this currency regime on the U.S economy have been clear for some years. Time is not on our side.

As CEOs and business leaders we get paid to deal with long-term issues. I am fortunate to have spent my career in a company that is synonymous with long-term thinking. But today American business and government lack a long-term, strategic clarity of thinking. It has become difficult for us to develop a consistent and coherent response to such challenges in the modern era of trade. We have the bureaucracy and the procedures of the World Trade Organization. We have the entanglements of free trade agreements. We have our competing political parties and their everlasting lust to squeeze one-sided political advantage from every situation. And on the business side we have the quick-buck artists and opportunists.

Do we have the willpower to draw a line in the sand against unfair trade? At what threshold of job losses and wealth erosion should we summon the nerve to change our policies — or at the very least our political posture?

Just a few years ago, in 2001, the United States government saw what was happening to the steel industry and decided to draw a line in the sand. President Bush announced a three-part Steel Action Plan to deal with a crisis that had developed in the industry.

First, under provisions of Section 201 of the Trade Act of 1974, the President requested that the U.S. International Trade Commission investigate whether the U.S. steel industry was suffering serious injury from a flood of imports. This was a much broader investigation than the specific issue I discussed earlier that involved just one category of steel from Brazil, Japan and Russia.

The investigation provided a sobering assessment of the industry. More than 30 American steel companies, representing 35 percent of our steel making capacity, had been driven to bankruptcy by the surge of imported steel, which included steel being "dumped" into the market below cost. More than 50,000 American steel jobs had been lost. By 2002 more than 50 percent of U.S. steel making capacity would be in bankruptcy. International Trade Commission members agreed unanimously that imports were a substantial cause, and only one member dissented in voting to recommend a tariff remedy.

A tariff is one way you draw a line in the sand. It is an excellent tool for containment. President Bush agreed with the International Trade Commission, and in 2002 he imposed tariffs and rate quotas on steel imports for a period of three years. It was a moderate and proportional response to the illegalities which led to the industry crisis.

The President had to buck a number of constituents in his own party and administration: the free trade true believers; those with a vested interest in the status quo; and those who have prostituted any rational definition of free trade in order to secure short-term gain. Also, I think to some extent his actions were something of a departure from his core beliefs on "free" trade.

That didn't prevent a political crossfire, and the administration took shots from the free trade advocates for taking a "protectionist" action and he also took fire for pandering for votes in traditional steel states. One of the major drawbacks in our current political climate is our unwillingness to agree on what is done on principle and what is done for politics.

Free trade with no conviction to enforce the rules mutually agreed upon is a disaster for our country.

The measures imposed by President Bush would provide American steel companies with some breathing room against the deluge of imported steel. They would also provide the opportunity to regroup. There was the public understanding that steel companies should take the opportunity to invest in equipment to reduce costs and enhance their competitive position, strengthen their finances and consolidate where necessary, bring capacity in line with the marketplace. In other words, the steel industry was expected to get its house in better order. The President's measures did not constitute some kind of protectionist bomb shelter. The mandate was clear: be ready for that day in 2005 when the Section 201 protections were set to expire.

For perspective it's important to note that the Section 201 protections had their limits. They did not apply to our NAFTA trading partners. They did not apply to 99 developing countries, and they applied only to certain kinds of steel products.

For additional perspective it's important to note that while the American steel industry was expected to "shape up" in the wake of these protections, there were no actions that the U.S. government could take to address the abuses that had prompted the tariffs in the first place.

As much as 85 percent of the steel made at that time outside the U.S. came from non-market economies or producers. These steel manufacturers benefited from subsidies, from domestic cartels or from government ownership. One estimate placed total subsidies from 1980 onward at more than $100 billion. Competitor's markets were protected by quotas, restrictive licensing agreements, mill-to-mill agreements and other anti-competitive mechanisms. The result was that the U.S. steel market was the most open steel market in the world: Ripe for the picking.

That was a fundamental trend that had brought the U.S. steel industry to a critical place: Even though demand was strong through the late 1990s, prices in the U.S. market were at 20-year lows.

President Bush's actions under Section 201 were fully justified and long overdue. But it is likely that the ink had not yet dried on his paperwork before some of our "trading partners" set to work to reverse the President's action. The European Union threatened retaliatory tariffs if the 201 protections were not removed, in spite of numerous special provisions that significantly exempted their products from tariffs. The term "trade war" started to pop up in meetings, press interviews and other forums.

The European Union's threat was seen as the potential opening round of a trade war. But the next step was the filing of a case with the World Trade Organization.

While our trading partners set about to dismantle the corrective 201 measures, the American steel industry worked very hard to consolidate, to invest, and restructure to become more efficient and competitive. Our trading partners' first success was realized when the World Trade Organization ruled that the U.S. tariffs and quotas constituted an illegal barrier to trade. Their second success came when President Bush responded to the WTO's decision by lifting the protections in December 2003, 16 months ahead of schedule.

To paraphrase an old Cold War story, we were eyeball-to-eyeball with the WTO over this issue — and we blinked. The niceties and complexities of foreign affairs and diplomacy can be frustrating for manufacturers when we must confront every day the illegal trade practices and deliberate distortion of markets by foreign manufacturers and their governments.

Take the Organization for Economic Cooperation and Development (OECD), a group of 30 countries that share a commitment to democratic government and market economies and which addresses a range of economic and social issues.

For years an OECD-sponsored group of major steel producing countries, has convened a series of meetings intended to curtail subsidies in the steel sector. After the seventh such meeting the group issued a communiqué stating that the group had reaffirmed its interest in reaching agreement. So they could agree that they still wanted to reach an agreement. Further the group stated that it agreed on some things but disagreed on others. Beyond that the group decided it needed to keep meeting.

And so it goes. These things can take years, and in the case of this undertaking they must ultimately wrestle with all of the clever ways that governments subsidize their steel industries, including, research and development subsidies, funding for environmental enhancements, financial support following natural disasters, tax incentives, tax holidays, taxes that are magically rebated at the border on exports, grants, loan guarantees, assumption of debts, and so forth.

There are plenty of "sticking points" in such negotiations, which often proceed at a leisurely pace that seems far removed from the urgency and headlong pace of the marketplace. North American steel manufacturers may face as much as 238 million tons of new steel production capacity coming on line from 2004 to 2008, and about 60 percent of that could be built in China, the government of which is heavily involved in subsidizing steel.

If the market is not ready to absorb 238 million tons of additional steel production capacity, and if a significant portion of that capacity receives unfair subsidies, then it is the unsubsidized, well-run companies in free markets that will be most seriously damaged.

Is it asking too much for our government to take a harder line against all the different forms of corruption in the international marketplace? I'm not calling for a one-size-fits-all strategy.

Yet while our responses may differ for different situations, our fundamental approach to trade should be firm, decisive and consistent. Was that not our intent with the 20th century's Cold War? As an American manufacturer it appears to me that the defining struggles and contests for the 21st century may be in the arena of international trade.

Perhaps Manufacturing Cold War is too strong a term. Some might argue that it is not strong enough — that we are in fact engaged in a kind of economic war. And perhaps either analogy could make people less willing to take a hard look at our situation and what is at stake.

But before we decide let's consider another term from the Cold War era. Remember the "Domino Theory?" That was the geopolitical idea that the fall of one nation to Communism could cause another nation to fall and so on, like a line of dominoes falling after just one was tipped.

For Americans, the Domino Theory and the Cold War have negative connotations — of a divisive issue and a difficult time. But we may need to face manufacturing issues with the sober realization that we are in fact engaged in a long-term, high-stakes struggle similar to the one we faced during the Cold War.

So the question remains: Are there potential domino effects if our manufacturing industries are closed and moved to foreign countries? With almost a decade of the largest manufacturing job losses in our history I believe this is a fair question.

One gratifying aspect of working in the steel industry is that people are always telling you how important you are to the country: "Steel is the backbone of our industrial system." When things get tough in the world of international trade, however, we find that we sometimes need to remind people just how important we are.

The other side of this coin is that steel manufacturers need other manufacturers to buy our steel. Where will American steel companies turn for customers if America manufactures fewer appliances and automobiles? Where will makers of American tanks and battleships purchase steel if we surrender our capacity to other countries? Or is America prepared to "outsource" our entire arms industry?

Consider titanium as a related example. We use it in aircraft and aircraft engines. We also use it to armor military vehicles, and it is used in the medical industry, including highly specialized prosthetics. It possesses qualities of strength and heat resistance that make it highly valued in many of these products. And like steel, American companies involved in the titanium industry have faced the dumping of imports into our markets at below production costs.

In 2003 the U.S. House of Representatives Armed Services Committee negotiated an extraordinary agreement with the Boeing Corporation in which the company committed to purchase a certain amount of American titanium in connection with certain defense contracts.

The idea behind the agreement was simple: Either shore up domestic commitments to purchase American titanium or risk losing the capacity to produce a metal that is crucial to our national defense.

Before you dismiss the idea that we could lose industries on a massive scale just consider the apparel industry. The U.S. Bureau of Labor Statistics projects that nearly 70 percent of all jobs in the apparel industry will have been lost in the decade 2002 to 2012. That is almost 250,000 jobs that were the backbone of their local economies and the best employment in their local communities.

I admit it: I get irritated when I hear people dismiss job losses of this magnitude. People are too quick to say that $9 an hour sewing machine operators in the U.S. cannot ever compete with Asian counterparts who work many more hours a day for pennies per hour. They see the $9 an hour figure as a measure of how "uncompetitive" the industry has become.

This ignores the billions of dollars that textile and apparel manufacturers have invested to make their industry productive. This ignores the industry's investment in a clean environment. It ignores the content of American wages that provide workers with a social safety net after retirement or in the event of disability.

Likewise, in speaking only of the "competitive" wages outside the U.S. this ignores the lack of workers rights and environmental protections (costs which we ultimately will address as part of a global environment).

But in considering the domino effect of shrinking manufacturing we should focus first and foremost on our own economy and our own communities. The pressure politics of globalists, internationalists and the free-trade-at-any-cost crowd try to make Americans feel guilty when we assert the idea that our economic security and national security should be a priority. It is important that Americans shift the balance of such politics so that patriotism, jobs and trade can be discussed with our national interests in mind — and requiring no apology.

We as a country spend decades negotiating trade agreements only to see very important provisions routinely abused because of a failure to enforce.

So where will the domino effect be felt when we lose manufacturing? First and foremost the middle class will feel the effects. Manufacturing is a cornerstone of the middle class economy, and it extends its benefits to those with college degrees, those without degrees, to black, white, rural and urban.

And as a nation of immigrants we should not forget that manufacturing has provided the first, second or third steps up the economic ladder for the people who come to our country seeking freedom and opportunity. Manufacturing has enabled immigrants from widely diverse cultures and nations to climb the ladder into the middle class.

If I could help Paul Revere prepare for his latter day ride I would tell him to ride through the middle class neighborhoods of America. If we continue to lose manufacturing capacity, it is our middle class neighborhoods that will bear the brunt of the damage.

The Economic Policy Institute reported in a Working Paper that 100 manufacturing jobs support 291 jobs in other

Making American Steel —
And Making American Steel Jobs

In the Late 1990s, the U.S. Steel Market was flooded by steel that was being illegally imported in violation of international trade laws. By 2002, 50 percent of U.S. steelmaking capacity was in bankruptcy, and more than 50,000 jobs were lost. Nucor workers continue to demonstrate that U.S. steelmakers can lead in technology, environmental responsibility and competitiveness.

The heart of Nucor's steel-making process is the electric arc furnace, which melts scrap steel by passing powerful electric currents through electrodes into the steel.

Molten steel that has solidified in the casting process is shown here in the "bend zone" of a billet caster. After making the bend from vertical to horizontal the billets will be straightened and cut to prescribed lengths.

Molten steel is cast into a variety of shapes in steel mills, including square or rectangular shapes called blooms or billets, and rolled into various diameters of "rounds," slabs of various thickness, sheet steel, beams, and other shapes.

These billets are ready to be used in the mill.

This giant steel ladle is being prepared for relining.

Nucor also manufactures steel joists and other products from its finished steel. These workers are assembling and welding joists at one of Nucor's Vulcraft plants.

Massive rolls are required to shape billets into a variety of products.

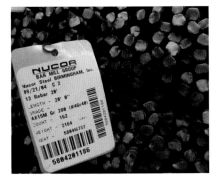

Many steel products are not seen in the final end use, such as this rebar, which will reinforce roads, concrete buildings, bridges and other structures across the U.S. Steel and other manufacturing components are often not seen by the general public, but add enormous strength to the U.S. economy.

Manufacturing workers are cornerstones of the American economy and their communities.

Making Our Message Loud and Clear to Washington, Beijing, and the World: Create a Level Playing Field for American Jobs!

Nucor has led an unprecedented grassroots campaign to strengthen U.S. manufacturing — calling for strong trade policy, energy self-reliance, and a broad domestic agenda to restore America's competitive position.

Across the nation, Nucor has hosted town hall meeting in support of U.S. manufacturing. At Nucor's Nebraska steel mill in August 2005, more than 3,000 local citizens turned out for the event, backing up traffic more than a mile from the plant gates.

At the Nebraska town hall meeting, this hot air balloon provided the headline and the call to action: "Save U.S. Jobs!"

Kirk Morgan provided an inspiring opening to the Nebraska town hall meeting by singing, "God Bless the U.S.A."

The North Carolina legislature, Nucor, and other concerned companies hosted internationally-known journalist, Lou Dobbs, who addressed political and business leaders in North Carolina concerning job losses, trade policy, and other issues confronting the United States.

CNN's Lou Dobbs and Nucor Chairman and CEO Dan DiMicco share thoughts about the loss of U.S. manufacturing jobs.

Nucor's town hall meetings have been well-attended by elected officials from both parties and from all levels of government. Here, U.S. Representative Joe Barton (left) is shown at the Texas town hall meeting with Jim Darsey, vice president and general manager of Nucor Steel Texas.

U.S. Senator Hillary Rodham Clinton addressed more than 1,500 citizens at the New York town hall meeting, stressing the need to deal with trade and other issues through an aggressive pro-manufacturing agenda.

New Yorkers attending the Nucor town hall meeting showed their support for U.S. manufacturing with an impromptu banner of their own.

Dan DiMicco, shown here addressing the Nebraska town hall meeting, has addressed crowds as large as 4,500 at Nucor's nationwide series of events. Several town hall meetings received national media coverage and were webcast.

Americans know that the issue of manufacturing jobs is grounded in patriotism, as well as national and economic security. This Nebraska veteran salutes the flag at the opening of the Nebraska town hall meeting

Old Glory was visible for quite a distance from Nucor's steel mill at the Nebraska town hall meeting.

parts of the economy, almost twice as much as the 154 jobs supported by the business services sector and more than three times the number of jobs supported by retail trade.

A big reason for this, the institute reports, is that manufacturers generate anywhere from twice the number to four times the number of jobs among suppliers. At Nucor we have a keen appreciation of this because we are a critical supplier for a variety of different manufacturing industries, including autos, machinery, heavy equipment and others. The Economic Policy Institute paper named autos, aerospace and primary metals as having some of the largest employment "multipliers."

The report concluded that "layoffs in the manufacturing sector tend to have much larger spillover effects in terms of indirect employment loss than layoffs in other sectors." As a result, the paper states, "These manufacturing job losses have had profound implications on the larger labor market of the United States, as indirect employment supported by these jobs have suffered as well."

Robeson County, North Carolina, provides a good example of what this suffering looks like across the United States. Largely rural, this county's 20th century history was one of slow but steady progress up from rural poverty and the Great Depression. Robeson County provided a noteworthy story of how blacks, whites and Lumbee Indians learned to live and work alongside each other as the local manufacturing economy grew.

Researchers from University of North Carolina at Pembroke and the Center for Community Action released a study in 2004 covering the years 1993-2003 that revealed the loss of $713 million in jobs, income and business taxes in this one county, resulting from manufacturing job losses during the period.

The county's economy suffered a stunning setback when its manufacturing base lost significant jobs to illegal competition and the flight of jobs to foreign countries. Communities like Robeson County are familiar to us at Nucor. In states as different as New York and Nebraska we operate steel recycling and manufacturing facilities in rural communities that will never be confused with New York City or Chicago as business, finance or industrial hubs. We learned long ago that manufacturing brings something very important to rural America, and that the small towns and cities repay our investment many times over. We have learned to value the productivity, the work ethic and the sense of community that our employees and their families share with their company. We value the people and their communities, and they value our investment and commitment to them.

So when I read about a place like Robeson County, where local manufacturing and the economy have been gutted, I can relate it very quickly to Nucor's nearby plants in South Carolina or North Carolina.

In 10 years, from 1993 to 2003 Robeson County lost more than 8,700 manufacturing jobs — from more than 17,000 to fewer than 7,000. In 2003 alone, nine plants closed. At the beginning of that period manufacturing accounted for 31 percent of the county's jobs. Ten years later that had dropped to only 18 percent.

84

As a result of those 8,700-plus lost jobs the region as a whole lost more than 18,300 jobs over ten years. Regional household income had dropped by $674 million per year. That is roughly two-thirds of a billion dollars lost to the regional economy. Rolled together it is a staggering number. But it is much more than a number. It is a story of hardship and loss for individuals and families who can not easily regain what they have lost.

The study indicates that this lost household income reflects losses to wages, salaries, benefits, retirement incomes, business proprietors and professionals such as doctors. The local hospital administrator was quoted, saying that the hospital had been reduced to running a deficit because it was providing more services than the patients could reimburse. The hospital was reduced to trying to cobble together grant money to help close the gap.

As the dominoes fell, local governments were not immune. By 2004 regional governments' collections of indirect business taxes had decreased by $39 million. These sales taxes, business taxes, excise and other taxes cannot simply be collected in another segment of a local economy that has been hit so hard.

In Robeson County during those years since 1993 more than 600 jobs were lost in education as a result of the manufacturing losses. More than 100 hospital jobs, almost 500 jobs in wholesale trade and another 475 jobs in motor freight were lost to the domino effect from lost manufacturing. Local banking suffered a net loss of almost 150 jobs, resulting in more than $13.6 million of lost income.

As we would expect, unemployment rates climbed steadily and peaked in 2001 and 2002. Unemployment insurance payments almost doubled just from 2000 to 2001. Robeson County unemployment rates tracked double the state level.

Personal bankruptcies nearly quadrupled since 1994, and increased steadily as the economy experienced a severe downturn from 1999 to 2002. As the county's economy lost manufacturing jobs its displaced workforce lost access to health insurance, and by 2002, three out of every ten people did not have access to health insurance. The infant mortality rate increased almost 2 percent from 1990 to 2000, which could also reflect this loss.

Taxpayer-funded benefits such as food stamps, Aid to Families with Dependent Children and other forms of assistance categorized as "income-maintenance benefits" shot up by $28 million from 1994 to 2001.

The authors of this report concluded, "Both the research model and findings are applicable to a significant number of rural counties across the United States that have experienced massive job loss over the past 10 years."

When Robeson County manufacturers fell victim to the huge economic forces that are assaulting the entire sector, the dominos fell for suppliers, truck drivers, government, health care, and most important, in the homes and lives of our fellow citizens.

This type of devastation has taken place across America due to the patently illegal practice of governments such as China. Am I ringing the bell unnecessarily or in an effort to impede free trade? Not hardly. In fact many businesses are waking up to the sad reality of our nation's failure to enforce important trade rules. And those that hide behind these abhorrent practices are at best greedy and short-sighted, and at worst un-American.

Hundreds of miles north of North Carolina The Public Policy Institute in 2002 published a report on the importance of manufacturing to Upstate New York. For New York State as a whole the manufacturing sector had a multiplier effect of 2.03, which meant that more than two jobs in the state's economy were created for every one job in manufacturing. In the Upstate, where manufacturing accounted for more than 17 percent of jobs the multiplier was 2.67, which meant that about one-half of all the region's jobs directly or indirectly linked to manufacturing.

The report discusses the "ripple effects from the generous benefits manufacturing jobs tend to provide." These include a list of things that go far beyond basic necessities to create what we recognize as a "quality of life:" foundation endowments, top-notch health care, quality schools and higher education, arts programs and civic programs.

The report sums up the economic equation this way: "Manufacturers export goods from their home area, and import the wealth earned by the sales." But it also points out that manufacturing is about more than standard of living. It is also about quality of life.

For many years New York has lost manufacturing jobs faster than the U.S. as a whole — anywhere from one-third to twice the rate of losses. Like other states New York is making sober (and sobering) assessments of its strengths and weaknesses. When people realize that 2.67 other jobs may be on the line for every single manufacturing job it forces tough questions to the fore. So officials in New York and elsewhere look at energy costs, and costs of government, and infrastructure and all of the elements that affect a region's ability to attract and retain manufacturing.

And it is not just because manufacturing is the goose that lays the economic golden egg. The Manufacturing Alliance of Connecticut publishes a yearly index covering a variety of statistics on the health of the state's manufacturers and their impacts on the people and the economy.

The index includes those basic statistics that help citizens and elected officials take stock of manufacturing's importance. For example, the 2004-2005 index reported that Connecticut's 211,442 manufacturing employees earned an annual payroll worth $10.3 billion and that they accounted for "value added" of $27.6 billion.

For each $1 million increase in sales generated by Connecticut manufacturers, all other industries realize additional sales of $2 million, and 11.6 new jobs are added to the economy, half of those in non-manufacturing sectors. There's a sales incentive in those figures that the whole state can share.

But the Connecticut report also brings to light another, crucial aspect of "value added." Six out of ten patents awarded in Connecticut are awarded to manufacturers, and this is in a state that is typically ranked among the top five in new patents per capita.

In the United States we are accustomed to seeing our-selves as the innovators. The steamboat, the telegraph, the Model T, the power grid, the airplane the personal computer

— we identify these breakthroughs with American ingenuity. The state of Connecticut shows us that this is still alive and well — and living in our factories and mills.

Are we really willing to walk away from this tradition? Are we willing to turn a blind eye to the consequences of losing our manufacturing edge? Of all the dominos to fall this one has the potential not only to devastate our economy but to change the fundamental way we see ourselves and to undermine the confidence and can-do spirit that have made Americans the most inventive people of modern times.

I began this chapter by raising the question of whether the competition between very different social and political systems has now moved to the manufacturing arena. I have touched on just a few of the dominos that we should think about in a "domino effect" similar to the concept originally developed for Cold War geopolitics.

Manufacturing as it has developed in the United States reflects some of the best of our democratic culture and society. From collective bargaining to self-directed work teams, American manufacturers have looked for better ways of negotiating and communicating across all levels. We owe this progress to our society, which values openness and participation. Nucor's own steel mill culture is built solidly on these values. I believe that when it comes to opening up opportunity for all kinds of people, manufacturing is one of the most democratic sectors in our society. People whose families have been here for generations work alongside immigrants. In Robeson County, North Carolina, blacks, whites and Lumbee Indians learned to work side by side in manufacturing in one of our country's most racially diverse rural counties.

People who have not, for whatever reason, taken the path of higher education can make above-average wages for their families, and they can discover outlets for their talents on the job. Manufacturers train and educate their employers, and for millions of workers this has been their higher education for a better life. It has proven an excellent path of upward mobility for people of every level of schooling. And for a nation of immigrants it has provided first, second generation Americans with their realization of the American Dream. If we lose manufacturing we lose an important economic ladder for immigrants.

The factory and the mill can reflect some of the best of our society and culture. But we have seen examples from China where its factories and mines reflect the worst of its culture: repression by authoritarian rule.

Again, I don't claim the U.S. is perfect. But we have the open, participatory society that roots out sweatshops and other labor violations. We have a free press in which citizens argue openly about the costs versus the benefits of regulations. Our laws are not just words on paper, they reflect the social compact that we have with one another, and they are created and enforced by a government that we ourselves elect. The lawmakers are answerable to all of us, including the factory workers, the miners and the political dissidents. We must insist that they move beyond words to action to enforce rules which allow free trade.

CHAPTER 4
LET'S STOP MERELY LECTURING THE THIEVES

For some, the dominos started falling for manufacturing in this country a long time ago, because we arrived at a place when many of us quit believing in factories and foundries and mills. For many of us, "factory jobs" and "smokestack industries" were no longer seen as a path to prosperity. They came to be regarded by some as the dirty, sweaty, mindless work of drudges — something not worthy of our educated, white-collar, suburban country.

If I could erase one phrase from our nation's mind-set I would have a hard time choosing between "post-industrial society" and "information society." I believe that those phrases, tossed around like other catch-phrases in our pop culture, continue to damage our nation's policies toward everything from regulation to international trade.

In 1973 Daniel Bell wrote his watershed book, "The Coming of the Post-Industrial Society." This is not a pop culture book. It is a scholarly, in-depth work, and Dr. Bell makes his points without resorting to sweeping statements. But it seems to me that the very title of his book has lodged in our minds and has profoundly shaped the way that we perceive our country and its economic landscape.

He wrote in 1973 that in the next "thirty to fifty years" we would see the emergence of what he called "the post-industrial society." Most of us have heard this term, and each of us probably has a personal picture of what this looks like. Factory workers are gone and replaced by cubicle dwellers. That's one vision of heaven, but not one shared by a steel guy. After all, somebody has to supply the steel for the office building that houses the cubicles.

Bell used other descriptions, including "the knowledge society, or the information society or the professional society. Basically this is what happens when we will move from a goods-producing economy to a service economy." In other words we won't make anything for each other any more, we'll all get rich moving information around and providing each other with services.

Now to be fair to Professor Bell he worked hard in this book to emphasize that he was not writing in absolute or sweeping terms. He used terms like "axis" to describe how "information" and "services" would become important lines along which we organize our economy and society.

In the old society, such things as capital (money for investment) and private property provided a main axis. But in the new post-industrial society such things as "theoretical knowledge" would become an important axis.

It disturbs me to read something like the following, which is quoted from the book: "most of the major industries of the nineteenth and early twentieth centuries — steel, telegraph, telephone, electricity, auto, aviation — were developed by talented tinkerers who worked independently of the fundamental work in science. . . ."

So there is my industry, the steel industry, relegated to the last century or the century before that, and beholden to tinkerers for its place in the world. And since we're looking at the previous two centuries, here is another quote: "In the nineteenth and early twentieth centuries the strength of nations was their industrial capacity, the chief index of which was steel production."

So here we are. First came the Stone Age, then the Bronze Age, then the Iron Age, then the Industrial Revolution, and now we don't need stone or bronze or iron or steel. Dr. Bell wrote: "In the post-industrial society, the chief problem is the organization of science, and the primary institution the university or the research institute where the work is carried out."

Let me weigh in here. Organizing science is your chief problem only if your electric grid and your transportation grid, and your construction industry and all of those other industrial things are plentiful, affordable and at your disposal. Take those out of the picture and your research institute is dark and deserted. Last time I checked, all of those things depended on steel.

With the year 2000 now a few years behind us it is always interesting to read predictions for that year. Bell predicted, "the entire area of blue collar work may have diminished so greatly that the term will lose its sociological meaning as new categories, more appropriate to the divisions of the new labor force, are established."

Most blue collar workers I know don't give a hoot that their work may lose its "sociological meaning." Their work has always meant steady pay, solid benefits, providing for their families and the satisfaction of making things.

Dr. Bell predicted the dominance of "the professional and technical class in the labor force" by 2000, and it is certainly fair to say that manufacturing's share of the labor force has diminished, probably much as he anticipated. My concern is

93

not the accuracy of his predictions or how we might argue his various points.

My concern is how such thinking affects the way we view our country and the kind of work we do as Americans.

Just nine years after Dr. Bell's lengthy, thoughtful book was published, John Naisbitt's best-seller, *Megatrends*, hit the market. Subtitled, *"Ten New Directions Transforming Our Lives,"* this book stands as a contrast to Bell's. Daniel Bell's book was expansive, geared to academics and serious students of his subject, although it did achieve success in the market and is still widely quoted. Naisbitt's book was geared to pop culture. In broad and sweeping terms he reinforced the idea that the "information society" was going to sweep aside a lot of old stuff that was cluttering the landscape and holding us back.

He described a society and economy in which "information" was placed squarely at the center, calling it the "strategic resource." He correctly anticipated the proliferation of computers and the use of technology to take over some skills that could best be described as repetitive and mechanical. U.S. industry has made huge strides in productivity for just this reason.

In recent years Nucor constructed and brought into commercial operation a steel plant based on a technology that had confounded steel manufacturers for almost a century and a half. The idea was simple: cast steel in thin sheets between two rollers. Why had no one been able to make steel using this simple idea? The knowledge and the technology sometime take a while to catch up with the basic idea.

Now, almost 150 years after the idea was first sketched on paper, we find that the steel industry is still a place where a breakthrough technology can create a better product and a lower cost, while requiring less energy in production and producing less greenhouse gases.

American manufacturers don't take a back seat to anyone when it comes to adapting technology. Even industries like steel know a good thing when we see one. We have invested billions of dollars of our old-fashioned capital in the information and the services and the technology to make us the most productive, environmentally friendly and safe steel mill that we can be. And we are not unique among American businesses. Our nation's textile manufacturers invested billions in boosting their productivity, and now we are asked to stand by while the entire industry is being decimated. Why? Maybe because the prophecy of an information economy has become self-fulfilling.

Why are Americans not more concerned about the loss of manufacturing? I believe that this post-industrial informa-tion-society school of thought is one big reason.

In 1982 John Naisbitt wrote: "We must put down our old industrial tasks and pick up the tasks of the future." And this, "Rather than reinvest in the industries that once made us great, we must move beyond the industrial tasks of the past, toward the great new enterprises of the future."

The last time I looked those "great new enterprises of the future" included minimum wage retail jobs and call centers. And if Nucor Corporation had heeded this advice to not reinvest in an industry that made us great, more than 11,000

Americans today would not have their good paying jobs with Nucor's steel mills.

This statement in Naisbitt's book caught my eye: "We are deeply in a process of a global redistribution of labor and production . . . . [T]he United States is yielding on apparel, steel and automobiles to Third World Countries." There is a lot of truth in that assessment, but it is precisely the kind of statement that should prompt us to stand up and say, "Not so fast."

First, we should assert that the United States does not "yield" anything that is precious — neither our freedoms nor our prosperity. Second, we should recognize that "Third World Countries" describes countries that traditionally could not make their own clothing, their own steel or their own automobiles to the same level of quality and quantity that we have achieved in the U.S.

So why should we be willing to yield the very industries on which we have built our wealth? According to the true believers in the "information society" or the "post-industrial society" we really don't need our factories and mills any more.

I disagree. We need them more than ever. Furthermore, we need to take a cold, hard look at this creeping, conventional wisdom about manufacturing. The unspoken assumption that steel mills are dinosaurs can lead to government policies that speed manufacturing's extinction in the U.S. They can result in trade policies that make the decline of manufacturing a foregone conclusion and self-fulfilling prophecy.

We therefore must confront this conventional wisdom, this sound bite from the seventies that sentences factory workers to joblessness and asks us to see manufacturing as some kind of relic from the 1800s. Whether we argue with academics in the universities or legislators in the halls of power it is time for the people who make things to stand and say that the "information society" just won't get the job done for us.

There is another, more fundamental reason for us to remain firm. I mentioned that manufacturing has been a door to upward mobility, open to all kinds of people from all walks of life. Many people have ambitions to move out of manufacturing, to move up to the kinds of jobs that Dr. Bell and John Naisbitt wrote about. I have known people at Nucor who have used their paychecks to educate their children for professions that are far away from the steel mill.

Nucor shares these ambitions, to the tune of more than $30 million to date. That's how much we have donated to college scholarships for Nucor employees and family members. Each Nucor teammate and dependant is eligible for $2,750 per year toward college or a vocational school.

But manufacturing is more than a stepping stone. Many college-educated people have chosen Nucor's steel recycling and manufacturing plants for their life's work. And many people whose education stopped at high school have made not only a good living for themselves, they have provided a high degree of security for their families.

Here is something that cubicle-dwellers and book writers may not know. There are people among us who enjoy and seek out jobs that only manufacturing can provide. We are drawn to the work and find satisfaction and reward in it. Personally, I love steel mills, and I have since the first day I walked into one.

After 30 years I am still in awe of steel making. If you have never been in a steel mill you have missed one of the most electrifying experiences on the planet. At Nucor we harness the elemental forces of electricity and heat and we apply it to discarded automobiles and other scrap steel. From these we forge steels that can hold up skyscrapers or shelter you from the rain. I once told someone that when you work in a steel mill you feel like you can take on the world.

And that's what American manufacturing has always done. We are not backward-looking. We are always among the first to incorporate new technology and new processes, and this has made our work increasingly challenging and satisfying. If we buy into the idea that we can build a post-industrial society or an information society then we are relegating millions of people to work that will not satisfy them or reward them in ways that "making things" can.

We like to make things. This is who we are. This is what we do. It's part of what makes us people. We like to work with our hands. At Nucor we enjoy bringing tons of scrap metal into one part of the plant and transforming it into useful steel products. It may be hard for outsiders to understand but the noise and the heat and the flame of it gets into our blood. And when we see those sheets and coils of glistening steel we know we have made something for our country, our families and ourselves.

If we write off manufacturing in this country as some kind of bygone relic, or as low-end, low-value work best done by cheap overseas labor then we effectively slam the door of opportunity in the faces of millions of people. And these are people who will find more satisfaction and more opportunity in manufacturing than they could possibly find in a pure information society.

We also slam the door on innovation. Like many human pursuits, manufacturing bridges the world of commerce with the realm of human creativity. The profit motive is a wonderful thing. It has made steel mills cleaner, safer, more efficient and — more profitable. At every step of the way the profit motive helped spur human creativity and innovation. Find a better way to make steel and we make a better profit.

Here in our wealthy, hard-working country we can see the results of this better-way-better-profit progression. We see the results in our homes and in our air-conditioned, safety-belted cars with state-of-the-art sound systems. Look carefully at the U.S. flights to the moon. In those moon shots were the dual legacies of pure science and profit-generated know-how. If we could trace all the connections we would see direct links between our highest and noblest achievements and the down-and-dirty business of manufacturing.

Manufacturing weaves not only a web of work and creativity, but a network for wealth to flow to all sectors of human endeavor — including other manufacturing. If we subtract manufacturing from our economy we risk losing the deep well of creativity and innovation that we need for our future well-being.

Here is an example. In 1965 Stephanie Kwolek and Herbert Blades created a remarkable fiber while working as research scientists at DuPont laboratories. They were

99

working with a family of fibers called aramids, which includes nylon. These organic fibers are entirely man-made. Their existence has sprung entirely from the imagination, the knowledge and the initiative of people such as Stephanie Kwolek and Herbert Blades.

This particular fiber proved to be light and yet it possessed a significant tensile strength. As a matter of fact it proved to be about five times stronger than the same weight of steel. (As steel makers we always take such comparisons as compliments.) It's called Kevlar, and today we recognize it as the lifesaving material that protects soldiers and law enforcement officers — because when woven with human ingenuity Kevlar is strong enough to stop a bullet.

Stephanie Kwolek obtained 28 patents during her distinguished 40-year career. Her knowledge and creativity were nurtured in laboratories that were themselves the product of our manufacturing economy. DuPont's sprawling and diverse manufacturing capabilities helped feed the knowledge and the financial resources into its laboratories, where scientists could perform such amazing feats as stopping bullets with something not much bigger than a spider's web.

But there's even more to Kevlar's manufacturing pedigree. Stephanie Kwolek earned her degree from the Carnegie Institute of Technology, now Carnegie Mellon University, in Pittsburgh.

Carnegie Mellon is described as "a pragmatic institution focused on finding real solutions to the problems facing society." The school describes its graduates as "the innovators and doers of their generation who made a difference in the world around them."

It was founded in 1900 as Carnegie Technical Schools, with a donation of $1 million by industrialist Andrew Carnegie. The university's early focus was on training and preparing students for work in industry. That's not surprising considering Carnegie had helped make Pittsburgh America's prime steelmaking city. The school expanded its degree programs and its focus to include research, and it was from that legacy that Stephanie Kwolek graduated in 1946. Kevlar would follow almost 20 years later.

Andrew Carnegie was a Scottish immigrant whose first job was as a bobbin boy in a cotton mill. He became one of America's leading industrialists, and expanded his iron and steel holdings to become the largest in the nation.

Carnegie funneled his fortune into libraries and schools, including the Carnegie Technical Schools. Steel mills created the wealth that funded the school that educated the woman who invented the fiber that was woven into the fabric that is five times stronger than Andrew Carnegie's steel — and can stop a bullet.

There is a thread that runs through our entire economy that ties together commercial success, prosperity, innovation, and scientific breakthrough. I am convinced beyond any doubt that if we allow our nation to go too far down the road of a "post-industrial society" that we will lose one of our society's most fundamental and important sources of inspiration. We need our factories as much as we need our schools.

Harvard economist Richard Freeman in a 2005 working paper published by the National Bureau of Economic Research, highlighted some trends that bear this out. He reported that U.S. pre-eminence in science and engineering is threatened by the offshoring of research and development to countries such as India and China. Also, companies from the U.S. and other developed countries are increasingly offshoring skilled work outside of research and development, even as developing countries close the technological gaps and export more high-tech products to the U.S.

What's noteworthy is Freeman's emphasis on what makes U.S. innovation and technological leadership inherently strong. These include the quality of our educational system, the close links between industry and our universities, government support for research and development, and corporate investment in research and development. When you consider corporate support of education and the government that means that American industry plays a role in all four of these areas. Subtract American manufacturing from the economy and you completely undermine the future of research and development (up to 60 percent of it is connected with manufacturing) and erase our technological edge.

But then, we don't always appear to support our technological edge with anything but lip service. I find it ironic and troubling that at the same time we toss around terms like "information society" and look down our noses at traditional industries we also allow international trade violators to do great damage to those areas of our economy that are truly "post-industrial."

Many U.S. trading partners are stealing our intellectual property, and they are doing it on a massive scale in a variety of industries.

Brazil is generally regarded as a U.S. ally and one of our most important trading partners in the Americas. Brazil is also on a special "watch list" of countries that do not adequately provide intellectual property protections. Brazil made the watch list by virtue of the fact that it is "one of the world's largest markets for pirated products."

Brazil's inadequate enforcement of laws against Internet piracy and "optical media piracy" (CDs, DVDs etc.) resulted in estimated losses exceeding $931 million in 2004. The U.S. Trade Representative report said that few Brazilian police raids in 2004 resulted in criminal prosecution and conviction. Also, Brazil's "ineffective border enforcement" leaves the market open to pirated and counterfeit goods.

Kuwait benefited from the armed intervention of a U.S.-led coalition to drive out an Iraqi occupation force. Yet in 2005 Kuwait joined Brazil on the priority watch list due to "its high rates of copyright piracy and its lack of progress in amending its copyright law to meet international obligations."

Kuwait continues to have "high levels of optical disc piracy" as well as problems with software, Internet and cable piracy. The U.S. Trade Representative report expresses the "hope" that "key ministries with IPR (intellectual property rights) enforcement responsibilities" will take "further measures to combat IPR infringement over the long term."

Such is the language of international diplomacy when applied to international trade violations. We

express our "hope" and then we schedule another meeting to "continue to address these issues."

If someone backed a truck up to one of Nucor's steel mills and tried to steal steel, we would have them arrested and prosecuted. Yet the United States posture in the arena of international trade seems to be one of patience, hope, and "discussions."

If we're going to tout the virtues of a "post-industrial society" shouldn't we make the full court press for enforcement of laws protecting all these post-industrial products?

From Lebanon comes the assessment of "rampant cable piracy, retail piracy of pre-recorded optical discs, computer software piracy and pharmaceutical counterfeiting." How many American jobs can be accounted for in that one sentence? Yet the U.S. Trade Representative report is full of sentences with, "We commend the Lebanese government. . ." and "We encourage Lebanon. . ." and "the United States urges Lebanon. . ." and again, "We encourage Lebanon. . ." and "We urge the Lebanese government. . ." and all of this is capped off with "We will continue to review Lebanon. . ."

Our trade posture is full of urges, encouragements and reviews. *That* will keep the bootleggers up at night. *That* will have the thieves looking over their shoulders.

Meanwhile, Russia's "extremely porous border," and "problematic IPR enforcement issues," result in a market where piracy and counterfeiting continue to rise through the roof. About 87 percent of software, 80 percent of movies, 73 percent of entertainment software and 66 percent of recordings are pirated and illegal. How much in lost wages and jobs does this represent? "Piracy in all copyright sectors continues unabated," the U.S. Trade Representative reported, "and the U.S. copyright industry estimated losses of $1.7 billion in 2004."

As with many other countries some raids are staged from time to time on plants where illegal products are made, but the report indicates that no plant licenses have been "permanently suspended" and that as much as 70 percent of seized pirated products are returned to the market. The famous line from the movie *Casablanca* comes to mind: "Round up the usual suspects."

The U.S. government responds with an urge. "We urge Russia to take immediate and effective steps. . ." et cetera, et cetera, and then follows with "We will continue to monitor Russia's progress. . ."

Progress? The rate of piracy is increasing? The level of piracy is above 80 percent for major product categories? Seventy percent of illegal goods gets returned to the market after confiscation? By all means, let us continue to monitor their progress.

Meanwhile, in China we find that "The United States remains gravely concerned" that China is not resolving "critical deficiencies" and "infringements remain at epidemic levels." The use of "gravely concerned" and "epidemic levels" is a tip-off. However bad things may be in Brazil, Lebanon, or Russia, the market in China must be in a league of its own.

Given that the United States imported more than $243 billion worth of Chinese goods while exporting only $41.8 billion worth of U.S. goods to China in 2005 it stands to reason that the theft of intellectual property in that country could be significant.

The U.S. Trade Representative reported that intellectual property rights infringement in China is at or above 90 percent for "virtually every form of intellectual property." That is worth repeating: piracy and rip-offs exceed 90 percent for virtually every form of intellectual property. It certainly makes the Russians look like amateurs.

When China was permitted to join the World Trade Organization back in 2001 it was expected to get its house in order for protecting intellectual property. The bad news is that China was not asked to get its house in order *before* joining the WTO. The worse news is that in some sectors piracy rates have actually increased since then.

Losses to the United States economy and its workers — just for piracy of copyrighted materials — approaches $3.8 billion per year. Here is a country that maintains a massive police state that can virtually snoop on every citizen's use of the Internet — and that can intervene in Internet usage to censor the World Wide Web, but it cannot muster its forces to enforce intellectual property rights. The irony of this is compounded by the U.S. Trade Representative's finding that in China Internet piracy is "quickly becoming the number one threat to the copyright industry. . . ."

But here is where the Chinese government adds insult to injury: The Chinese are exporting pirated goods to the U.S. so that we are buying the very products that are doing economic damage to our economy. One must give grudging credit to the Chinese: There appears to be nothing that they can't export to the U.S. By 2004 more than two-thirds of U.S. Customs' seizures in this category were from China.

Pharmaceutical companies selling into the Chinese market lose anywhere from 10 percent to 15 percent of their revenues, and the rate is going up.

The U.S. Trade Representative's report outlines the various reasons that the Communist government of China has managed to let this one small aspect of Chinese life slip outside its grip. The government has put laws on the books but enforcement is "seriously inadequate." Everything from protectionism to corruption plays into this, with the result that infringements go well beyond the typical movies and software to include pharmaceuticals, chemicals, information technology, textile fabrics, floor coverings, consumer goods, electrical equipment, automotive parts and industrial products, "among many others."

How many jobs and lost wages are represented by the information summarized above?

Not to worry. The Chinese government announced a crackdown in 2004. It was a thoughtful act indeed to announce it in advance, and to further advise the criminals that the crackdown would end after one year, in August of 2005. But then in March an official extended the program until the end of 2005. By then it should all be taken care of. Also in 2004 the Communist government launched an "awareness campaign" and broadcast a television special, on state-run TV. In February 2005 the government put on an "anti-piracy" concert in Beijing that was supposedly seen by a television audience of 500 million.

For the concert, the TV shows and other ineffective actions, the U.S. Trade Representative report said this: "The United States reaffirms its appreciation for the efforts of Vice Premier Wu Yi and the progress that has been made in some areas."

We as a country need more than "progress" we need conviction. To enforce a system of trade laws that provides mutual protections.

"Progress" is apparently defined in China as it is in Russia. Beyond that the U.S. government is pressing ahead to address the issues through various World Trade Organization mechanisms, and has put China on its "watch list." It is calling on the Chinese government to take "aggressive action" and to demonstrate increases in the numbers of investigations, prosecutions, convictions and deterrent sentences. The government is further called on to "demonstrate a significant decline in exports of IPR infringing goods." That would be a good first step. If Americans are going to buy products from China they should be assured that they are legal.

The problem is huge, and it is global. In 2005 one of every three music CDs sold in the world was an illegal copy, according to the International Federation of Phonographic Industries. In 31 countries, sales of illegal CDs exceeded legal sales. In Paraguay 99 percent of CDs were illegal and the country was a major transshipment point for blank discs to other South American countries.

In 2002 "copyright industries" contributed more than $625 billion to the U.S. gross domestic product and were responsible for 5.5 million jobs. More than 50 percent of their revenues come from outside the U.S., and it appears to me that the general lawlessness of global markets makes it obvious that the losses are almost impossible to measure. The International Intellectual Property Alliance estimated in 2005 the global losses to these industries at between $25 billion to $30 billion. The Alliance has focused particular attention on China and Russia.

The National Association of Manufacturers testified before the U.S. Congress that counterfeit products are particularly damaging to small and medium-sized manufacturers, which are losing market share to illegal products from China and elsewhere. In its testimony the association produced a Chinese counterfeit of an American product that included not only the counterfeit product but packaging and even a counterfeit product warranty.

Small manufacturers can be placed in desperate circumstances by such counterfeits, and the time it takes for a business to be destroyed is much less than the time it takes for governments to negotiate trade agreements and agree on corrective actions. It seems to me that time is often on the side of the counterfeiters and other trade criminals.

If time is not on our side why do we not see more urgency? Given what we have invested in the post-industrial economy, and given our potential rewards, I am at a loss to understand why we as a people and our government are not more upset about what is happening (or not happening) in the area of intellectual property rights. If the "information society" is our 21st century bread and butter why do we not take more forceful and timely actions to protect it?

To be fair, at least part of the fault may lie in our own culture. Perhaps it is because our idea of crime in general and theft in particular has not made the leap to the information society.

We often associate intellectual property theft with rich entertainers or big rich corporations, and we perceive small transactions as downloading music or buying knock-off products as "not a big deal in the big scheme of things."

But it is a big deal, and if we are serious about making our living in this post-industrial- information-age world of ours we must learn to reckon with the true costs of theft, counterfeiting and piracy. We must all come to respect intellectual property rights, and we must put in place laws that work and enforce those laws to the best of our ability.

We in the steel industry have spoken out for years in support of stronger trade policies and more effective enforcement. As we look around our economy today we see the evidence that weak policies and ineffective enforcement do not leave any segment of our economy undamaged.

We should not allow the globalization of our economy to dull our sense of these violations. I have already mentioned that free trade agreements such as NAFTA change our sense of "we" and "us" because the countries involved band together to carve out a new sphere of mutual interest in the larger world.

Also, the emergence of multinational companies and the globalization of revenues can blur the traditional lines of self-interest and the traditional way we define "us." A purely Brazilian company may strongly identify its interests with that of its home country. But a company that is equally rooted in Brazil and Hong Kong may see its interests in a different way. American companies whose revenues come primarily from overseas markets can be expected to view international trade issues from a different perspective of self-interest.

IndustryWeek publishes an interesting report on the geographic breakdown of company revenues among U.S. manufacturers. Its 2004 report noted that Fairchild Semiconductor, headquartered in Maine, generated about 85 percent of its total sales outside the U.S. IndustryWeek characterized the computer and electronics industry as "the most global major industrial sector by a long shot" and reported that about 60 percent of its sales came from international markets.

In contrast, the paper, petroleum & coal and furniture & fixtures segments all had less than 20 percent of their sales from international markets, on average. The report highlighted "globalization leaders" in various industry categories and these included familiar names to American consumers, including Coca-Cola, with 74 percent international sales, Tupperware, with 73 percent international sales and Gillette, with 63 percent international sales.

Americans — as consumers, shareholders and employees — have become accustomed to the multinational business landscape. Our shelves are stocked with its products and our parking lots are filled with its cars, trucks and SUVs. Everything from electronics to gasoline has a multinational pedigree.

Multinational companies by definition operate in "more than one country" but it would be difficult to find a true multinational today that operates in just two as opposed to 22. Multinationals typically don't just sell in all of these countries, they build and operate plants, they establish joint ventures and partnerships, and they buy companies or controlling interests in foreign companies outright.

The U.S. Bureau of Economic Analysis reports that in 2003 U.S. multinational companies employed 21.8 million people in the U.S. and 8.4 million outside the U.S. by majority-owned foreign affiliates. About one in five American workers in private industry were employed by U.S. multinational parent companies.

Another 5.2 million U.S. workers were employed by majority-owned U.S. affiliates of foreign multinational corporations. I spent my career with a U.S.-based company with most of its facilities in the U.S. Since 1988 Nucor Yamato Steel has manufactured steel beams at our facility in Arkansas. This is a partnership of Nucor Corporation and Yamato Kogyo Company Ltd. of Japan. Although our facility is in Arkansas, clearly our business relationship with a Japanese company begins to influence our thinking, and redefine the scope of our interests.

Nucor's international strategies can be characterized as conservative, relying on joint-venture partnerships and seeking to harness advanced technologies to "leapfrog" traditional manufacturing technology and create a clear advantage in the global marketplace. We do not want to advance an international strategy that just puts pins on a map or that do not advance the interests of our U.S.-based business.

One example is in Australia where we have established a joint venture project with Rio Tinto (Australia), Mitsubishi (Japan), and Shougang International (China). This facility will advance a technology called Hismelt, which converts iron ore into liquid metal and eliminates the need for coke ovens and other traditional steps in the iron-making process. It is a much more environmentally friendly pig iron production process than those used traditionally.

In Brazil Nucor's joint venture with Cia Vale do Rio Doce is advancing a technology that produces pig iron through a revolutionary fuel chain that begins with cultivated eucalyptus trees. Using an 89,000-acre tree plantation to produce its fuel the plant will be virtually self-reliant for energy. By replacing fossil fuels with this renewable resource we can produce pig iron for steel production while helping reduce the release of greenhouse gases.

These projects represent "overseas" businesses for Nucor, but they ultimately strengthen our U.S. operations while expanding the scope and reach of our business. We recognize that businesses today must diversify their geographic base, but we do not necessarily see it as a zero sum game for U.S. workers.

At Nucor we cannot predict the direction and ultimate scope of our business around the world. Likewise, we cannot predict how this will shape the way our workers perceive their company and their place in the global economy as we expand and change.

Foreign affiliates of multinational companies account for a significantly growing portion of international trade. McKinsey & Company reported that in 1990 these foreign affiliates accounted for $31 billion of the U.S. trade deficit. This figure more than doubled in just seven years, then doubled again in five years.

It is well established by now that many of multinational companies are seeking to lower their labor and other costs by a big margin. According to McKinsey & Company this "has had a disproportionately large impact on the foreign affiliate trade balance." In other words, it is not only our companies that are moving offshore, it is our wealth.

Imports from these affiliates are growing at a faster pace than from more established and developed countries — a direct result of the rapid growth of our investment in these low-cost, developing economies. It is pointed out that as U.S. companies earn more money from these foreign affiliates they have more to invest in new plants, new technology and thereby create economic growth.

But the astounding fact is that more than 40 percent of what we import to the United States is imported by the overseas subsidiaries of American companies.

We are told that foreign affiliates of U.S. multinationals are generating wealth for the U.S. but they are responsible for about one-third of our current account deficit (the wealth flowing out of our country). If we were to take a purely egalitarian viewpoint we would be justified in asking American executives of multi-nationals if they are willing to see their salaries reduced to a more "competitive" level, equal to say, the average executive pay in China or Guatemala.

We could conduct studies to see how the salaries and fringe benefits of government officials, consultants and economists in our country could be brought into a competitive parity with their third-world counterparts.

But my point is not to throw stones at American companies that are trying to survive and compete in global markets. The larger question is similar to the ones raised by NAFTA and CAFTA and the global economy in general: How do we define "us"? How do we establish what our own best interests may be? When does the private pecuniary interest of a multi-national conflict with its nation's interest? **The answer here must be in enforcement of rules designed to establish free trade.**

In a market where borders are increasingly irrelevant how do we know where to draw the line when it comes to the rules of the game?

The perspective of the American worker is beginning to shift on such issues. It is projected that up to 3.3 million U.S. jobs may move offshore by 2015. If you are a "multinational" you may have no sense of having left one place to go to another. The world may be your market and you may feel it right to obtain your resources (human and otherwise) in the location that is best for your business.

But if you are an American worker, employed by a company with a familiar American name on the door, it doesn't feel "multinational" when the jobs are shipped to India or China or the Philippines. It feels like those jobs have been taken from "us" and moved to a foreign country.

Today American workers are beginning to ask, "Who will be left standing?"

When the factory jobs started to dwindle in number some people said, "Good riddance." The jobs were dirty and back-breaking and relics from the nineteenth century. (Some said.) And besides, it didn't affect very many people. (Some thought.) If the old rust-bucket plant closed then it was just the natural order of things — even if the jobs ultimately left the country. (Some believed.)

Besides, everyone was pointing to the post-industrial society where happy workers would process, move, deliver and digest ever growing amounts of information. So as we watched millions of factory jobs head overseas we didn't hear much outcry from the post-industrial crowd. Then they began to get a little insecure because the multinationals and others began offshoring all of those "post-industrial" jobs to foreign countries.

Suddenly it's not just the blue collar jobs moving out. The great exodus now includes jobs such as software developers and call centers that stand as proud examples of the post-industrial professions. For the first time since Daniel Bell's book and John Naisbitt's follow-up, we have begun to doubt some of the rosier assumptions about wealth and the information society. No one anticipated this would give us indigestion in the workplace.

Now some Americans face a scenario they thought unlikely: Unemployment in the very businesses that were supposed to replace the factories. What happens when we arrive at the post-post-industrial society?

There is an old Italian proverb, *"Siccome la casa brucia, riscaldiamoci."* Loosely translated it means, "As long as the house is on fire we might as well warm ourselves." I believe that proverb expresses a widespread, unspoken attitude of our culture and society toward manufacturing.

With so many people working in service industries and other parts of the economy, manufacturing is not the "house" in which most of us live. Also, manufacturing is not the house of the post-industrial future. So even as we began to perceive that the manufacturing house was burning down we didn't get too upset. Might as well warm our hands by the fire.

But now, with offshoring and outsourcing of the new information age jobs, people are suddenly getting alarmed. The sparks have jumped to the roof of the house next door. Someone should call the fire department. Someone should do something about these violations and illegal competition!

As someone from the old-time industry, about all I can say to my colleagues from the post-industrial society is this: "Welcome to my world."

CHAPTER 5

WE ARE HOLDING SOME OF THE WRENCHES
BEING USED TO DISMANTLE U.S. MANUFACTURING

To this point you might think I am a pessimist. I'm not, and here's why. At the beginning of the American Revolution the colonists didn't know that they could whip the British. They just knew that they were tired of being held back by the old economic order and by the tyranny of the English king.

America's manufacturing industries today know that they can compete with the best of them when the playing field is level and the rules are enforced. Throughout my career I have seen one American industry after another retool, reinvent and revolutionize itself, whenever the market raised the bar.

If America allows too much of its manufacturing base to be pulled out of the country we risk losing our fundamental capacity to make things. When we lose that fundamental capacity we risk losing the fundamental capability to reinvent ourselves and our economy.

Nucor fundamentally reinvented itself almost a half century ago. Steel began as a sideline for us at a time when our focus was instruments and technology for the nuclear industry. At a crucial point in the company's history we shifted our focus to steel, because we saw opportunity and because we saw that we could be both strong and innovative.

That was in the 1960s when the U.S. steel industry was dominated by the big, traditional "integrated" steel mills. Integrated steel mills make steel from the most basic ingredients, including iron ore and coke. You might call it "steel from scratch." The steel industry at that time had many characteristics of "Big Steel," with high labor costs and aging facilities that depended on old technology and hardware. The American steel industry had become the world's biggest and wealthiest, but it was riddled with hidden rust on its facilities, its business model and its all-round approach to making steel.

It was the perfect time for a small, nimble competitor to revolutionize and reinvent the industry.

Nucor did not set out to reinvent the steel industry. We were just trying to find a better, cheaper way to make steel, when we learned about electric arc furnaces. With this kind of furnace, a powerful electric current heats scrap steel for manufacturing new steel products. Nucor took the chance on this underdeveloped technology and began operating its first electric arc furnace mill in 1969. Because of the risks that Nucor took, electric arc furnace technology today accounts for about half of U.S. production. As a result, no other industry compares with steel in its reliance on recycling.

But at the time Nucor adopted the electric arc furnace there were two common reactions to the technology and the business model. Skeptics said it was impractical. "Big Steel" said it was no threat to the big, old, integrated mills. Both were wrong. Nucor benefited from being a "first mover" with the electric arc furnace, but steel purchasers benefited also. The market rewards are obvious. Because of our dynamic, open and market-driven economy Nucor has become the second largest U.S. steel producer and the world's largest recycler.

Revolution did not scare us then, and it does not scare us now. And that is true of America's manufacturers in general. When we raise concerns about currency manipulation, labor rights abuses, reliance on polluting, deadly, subsidized energy resources and other illegal and unfair short-cuts we do it for many reasons — but not because we are afraid to compete.

The U.S. textile industry is often held up as an anti-competitive industry trying to hide behind protectionism. But this industry invested more than $2 billion per year from the early 1990s through the turn of this century, and drove up its productivity by 165 percent. In 1975 each loom on average produced 8 square yards of cloth, and by 2003 the average had been increased to 41 square yards.

That is not the behavior of an industry in retreat from competition. And when textile companies and steel companies join together to protest currency manipulation, import dumping, sweatshop factories, and wages that don't provide basic subsistence then their actions should not be dismissed as "protectionist."

Free trade at any cost believers are quick to slap the protectionist label on American industries when we speak out for enforcement of fair trade. These same critics often fail to appreciate the investment of money and effort that these same American industries have made to reinvent themselves, to revolutionize their business, and to compete in the global markets.

The "protectionist" label hurts us twice. First, it narrows our motives to account only for self-interest. Second, it is backward-looking. "Protectionist" implies that American companies seek to return to a more sheltered market — that they are unwilling and unable to undergo the significant change and pain required to compete.

I defy anyone to make "protectionist" stick to Nucor. There has not been a single aspect of our business that we have been unwilling to change in order to compete. When we underwent our revolution it did not stop with the electric arc furnace. That launched our success, but the rest of it has come with questioning virtually every assumption and conventional wisdom that we might have inherited from our own past or from the steel industry.

For example, we completely scrapped the type of organization that was typical of most steel companies and other American industrials at the time. Even as our company doubled in size and doubled again we did not add layers of management and corporate departments. Here's how: We hire talented people, train them and empower them to make decisions and to innovate. Not surprisingly our ranks produce innovative, quick-thinking division general managers and we reward them with a high degree of autonomy.

Only two layers of management (at most) separate hourly employees from their top management at our various mills and production facilities. And the organization has only four layers from the workers to the CEO. Any employee can speak directly to the president at any time.

Our first principle of employee relations is that we give them the opportunity to earn more as their productivity rises. And guess what — both their productivity and their paychecks are among the best in our business or any other business. And their workplaces are the total opposite of oppressive, sweatshop industrial workplaces.

This instills in Nucor workers the confidence that if we all do our jobs well then we will continue to have jobs tomorrow. Our people do not feel the need for protectionism, but they rightly expect their government to cede no unfair advantage to any competitor.

When Nucor employees look overseas at pollution-belching steel mills that would be outlawed in the U.S. they see both an unfair competitive advantage and harm to their own environment. They see a plant that undercuts their company's investment in state-of-the-art continuous emissions monitoring equipment. They are justifiably proud that their company leads the steel industry in the use of this technology, but would be justifiably outraged if a polluting overseas plant were able to turn our state-of-the-art pollution controls into a competitive disadvantage due to higher costs.

Nucor employees know that by recycling steel their plants consume much less energy to produce a ton of steel. Combined, Nucor's plants save enough energy in one year to power Los Angeles for eight years. When it is time to compute the dollar value of American manufacturing in the world economy we should calculate the value of energy saved and pollution prevented.

This high degree of efficiency, environmental stewardship and wealth creation has all been created in an open, free-market society. Workers rights are enforced in an open, representative, equitable system of government. Environmental protections are part of the social contract, willingly created by the government through the consent of the governed. Hard work, productivity, innovation and risk-taking are all rewarded, and the rewards are shared.

Nucor's story, and those of many other American manufacturers are not stories of American perfection, they are stories of American struggle and progress. Free societies inherently do a better job of reinventing or revolutionizing themselves. The same can be said for industries in those societies. What's more, I believe the benefits flow more freely and more swiftly to society as a whole.

If world prosperity and freedom are to be taken to the next level then it is important that the various levers and pulleys of international trade agreements do not undermine what we have achieved and built so far. We should never allow low-cost, polluting, sweatshop manufacturers in repressive societies to undercut and undermine the higher standards that we have achieved in more developed economies. If international trade agreements and weak U.S. foreign policy undermine American manufacturers, we have the potential to sacrifice much more than jobs.

We must bring a realistic assessment and a realpolitik to the distinction between free trade and managed trade. The plain fact of the matter is that governments use a variety of tools to manage trade to the advantage of their industries, suppliers and raw materials producers. They erect all kinds of structural barriers within their markets to discourage access by competitors or to discourage the export of raw materials to competitors.

They insinuate exceptions into everything from tariff reductions to subsidy disciplines, and free trade suffers death by a thousand small strokes, replaced by something that can more accurately be called managed trade.

Such actions subvert free trade and in a strong sense make it a convenient fiction. Every true believer in free trade should understand the true nature of the system that currently bears the name "Free Trade." And we should recognize it for the fiction that it has become.

For these reasons we must make a strong case that the advancement of American manufacturing is not "protectionism." We have demonstrated clearly that we can compete by investing in technology, by creating new products, by boosting productivity and by delivering the highest quality products with the least environmental impacts.

We are advancing our world's economy in the manner that it should be advanced. The international trade bureaucrats and career diplomats will not confront this ugly fact: Unfair trade practices which fail to enforce reasoned terms often benefit the countries and industries with the poorest environmental and human rights records.

The various international diplomatic and trade organizations are also full of politicians and bureaucrats who want to use various international agreements as tools of wealth redistribution. Woven through the Kyoto Protocol and in the World Trade Organization are requirements that developed nations operate under more restrictive and high cost regulations while allowing developing nations and least developed nations to operate at lower standards (and lower costs).

It may be fair at some level to ask a rich country to spend more on the environment. But if you end up shutting down the cleaner, more progressive industries in the developed countries, what have you accomplished? And many of these requirements end up being anti-competitive and even anti-American. It is not "protectionist" to make the distinction, and it is not "protectionist" to insist on the enforcement of trade agreements such that they do not siphon off our industries.

The plain fact is that we need manufacturing to continue to create wealth and economic opportunity for our own people.

If we are going to make a better future for our country we must continue to make things in our country. We have the can-do attitude. We have the technical prowess. We have the economic power. We have the best workers. We have the cleanest factories and energy facilities. We have the culture and the people that gave the world the steamboat, the telegraph, the Model T, the telephone, the television, the personal computer and the power grid.

What we need now is this vision: That the 21st century will be a greater century for American manufacturing than the century before it. We should be as committed to that idea as we are to our national security. And we should be committed to getting it done in the rough and tumble of the business and political worlds.

When we peel back the layers of our vision, here's what we see. We see a future in which

- All employers trading in the world market are held to high and equitable standards.

126

- All producers commit the same resources to achieve comparable levels of environmental protection.
- Where no government is allowed to own, subsidize or control the means of production to the detriment of free-market competitors.
- Where international agreements are enforced fully and fairly — not only regarding specific trade actions but also with regard to broader government policies such as currency and other economic intervention.

But there is another component of this vision. The United States must get our own house in order. We must ask tough questions. Are we shooting ourselves in the foot and contributing to the movement of manufacturing jobs and capabilities out of our country? The plain fact of the matter is this: We ourselves are holding some of the wrenches being used to dismantle American manufacturing.

Like the goose that laid the golden egg our own government has looked at manufacturers as a never-ending source of wealth that can be mined for tax revenues, mandated benefits, social engineering legislation, noble (and expensive) environmental mandates and the general funding of our massive government burden.

One reason for this is the skewed perception that politicians, activist groups and others have of manufacturing. They often characterize us as big corporations with deep pockets and thousands of employees. Many U.S. manufacturers are household names, and they are associated with highly successful products, decades of economic success and with the traditional U.S. dominance in the global economy.

Nothing could be further from the truth. The National Association of Manufacturers reported earlier in this decade that small to medium size manufacturers comprise about 95 percent of all U.S. manufacturing firms and employ about half of U.S. manufacturing employees.

Small manufacturers employ fewer than 500 people, and medium size manufacturers are defined as those with fewer than 2,000 workers. They account for about three-fourths of the new jobs created each year in the sector, and just like their larger counterparts they create jobs that pay above average — in this case about 20 percent more than other types of small business.

Every tax, every regulation, every government mandate has a cost that is placed squarely on the back of the company being taxed, regulated or conscripted to put the mandate into action. A cost-benefit analysis will show that sometimes the benefits flow back to the company. A cost-benefit analysis may also show that there is no clear-cut benefit, and in fact quite the opposite may be true.

The trick is to know how those costs and benefits flow into the economy and how they help us or hurt us.

As a manufacturer himself I believe that Paul Revere today would be leading the call for a completely fresh look at how taxes, regulations and government mandates are whittling away at our manufacturing base and its jobs. I'm reminded of the old saying, "The road to hell is paved with good intentions."

In a watershed study commissioned by the National Association of Manufacturers and the Manufacturers Alliance, economist Jeremy Leonard determined that the

U.S. manufacturing sector "labors under a 22.4 percent cost burden" imposed on it through taxes, health and pension benefits, tort litigation, regulation and rising energy prices. In other words those five components of our society and our economy are adding almost 25 percent to the basic cost of making things in this country.

Another way of saying it is that we are handing a 22.4 percent competitive advantage to every competitor in the world — outside the United States.

This study was not a Trojan Horse to justify the stripping away of benefits, the gutting of our legal system or to equip industry to avoid its fair share of taxes. It was, however, a legitimate wake-up call to the American people — that everything has a price. If we insist on taxing manufacturers at a certain level, if we insist on mandating certain benefits, if we insist on requiring certain pollution controls, if we insist on letting frivolous lawsuits continue at their current level then we will pay a price.

Now in a closed system, we could simply pass those higher costs on to consumers through higher prices. But in this era of globalism this cannot be done.

And this is where the globalists get real quiet. Here is where we point out that our tax burdens, our regulatory mandates and our lawsuits no longer affect just "Fortress America." It's no longer a closed loop where we can expect our fellow Americans to swallow the costs. We are discovering that the global economy is very unforgiving when it comes to higher costs.

For every American industry struggling with higher costs imposed by its own government and its own economic system there is a foreign competitor that is willing to seize the advantage. And given the speed of global communications and the sophistication of global shipping and logistics many companies can now price, manufacture and deliver the goods as swiftly from the far side of the world as the Americans can from just down the road.

If we are going to strip away every advantage of Fortress America then we must also strip away every disadvantage we impose on ourselves.

In his report Mr. Leonard stated that these cost burdens that we have imposed on ourselves have offset much of the unprecedented gains made by U.S. manufacturing since 1990. Think of what this means. All of our investment in new plants, all of our technological leaps forward, all of our efforts to squeeze the most value out of our manufacturing process — all of this was completely negated by self-imposed costs related to taxes, regulations, lawsuits and our incoherent energy policies.

(And I am compelled here to add that all of our hard work has also been negated by the currency manipulation, subsidies, dumping and other illegal practices of our trading partners.)

The report noted that U.S. industry spends more on pollution abatement than the so-called "green" trading partners in Europe. This is particularly annoying to some Americans because European politicians are often quick to criticize U.S. policy on Kyoto Protocols and other high-profile issues. It appears they may be less quick to impose costs on their industries. Perhaps they are more competitive minded than they are "green."

Another important point that surfaced in the wake of this report was the idea that U.S. manufacturing wages cannot be singled out for blame when we lose the competitive advantage. On wages alone U.S. industries are often very competitive because we have achieved high levels of productivity across a wide range of industries.

The NAM and Mr. Leonard have made it abundantly clear: We must account for any and all costs that put American manufacturers at a disadvantage and put our workers at risk. If our government is responsible for policies that ultimately put our workers at risk then we should be bold enough and honest enough to step forward and address the problems — now.

Capital is the lifeblood of manufacturing. U.S. steelmakers, unlike their Chinese counterparts, cannot count on the government to throw unlimited money at building our industry. We require the investment of capital, and we require a business environment in which that risk and that investment are rewarded if the business performs.

But in the U.S. we tax capital more than almost any other industrial democracy, and we often tax it more than once. Our corporate tax rates are not competitive. What's worse, we have no clear competitive philosophy behind our tax system. When the U.S. government finally extended tax credits to research and development it could not see its way clear to make the credits permanent. Even as our manufacturing base continues to erode we have not created a coherent and comprehensive strategy for taxation and regulation.

An entire generation has grown up and entered the workforce since the Energy Crisis of the 1970s and we have yet to develop a coherent and comprehensive policy to increase domestic energy supplies. If you want an example of a "lost generation" in American politics I will point you toward energy policy. The NAM study pointed to the unnecessarily high cost of natural gas in this country because we lack the leadership, the willpower, the urgency and the conviction to tap our resources and develop our infrastructure.

Meanwhile, the mechanisms used elsewhere to carve out unfair advantages create the illusion of lower costs. If the markets were allowed to work freely with many of our competitors then the illusion of lower costs (manipulated costs, actually) would vanish. The true low-cost producers, with the true comparative advantage, would emerge.

But in the meantime, their artificial advantages, combined with our self-imposed disadvantages combine to work against us.

We have also painted ourselves into a corner because we ask our government to spend more than it earns. We get trapped by our budget deficits into thinking that we cannot give "big business" a "tax break" because "we" (the government) need it. At some point we have to cut spending enough to get the deficit monkey off our backs.

It is well and good to say we "need" the money that we get from taxing industry to fund our various government departments, entitlement programs, national defense etc. But we have arrived at the point where we "need" more money than we can squeeze out of our industry and it is still not enough — to the tune of hundreds of billions of dollars.

Meanwhile, our competitors are equipping their Industries to operate more cheaply and more competitively.

Consider these highlights from the NAM study:

- Every major trading partner except Japan taxed corporations at a lower rate than we do.
- Every major trading partner except Germany, South Korea and France benefited from lower employee benefits costs.
- In every trading partner where the systems could be compared, all had lower tort costs (lawsuits etc.).
- The industries of Canada, Japan, Germany, the U.K, and France all benefit from a cost advantage for pollution abatement.
- The calculated disadvantage for U.S. workers is equivalent to adding a cost of $5 to every hour worked by every manufacturing employee in our country. That's $5 per person per hour for every hour worked.

Clearly, this is one area where America must demonstrate its talent for reinventing itself. I said at the beginning of the chapter that free and open societies can accomplish this more swiftly and more effectively than closed, oppressed societies. It's time for us to prove this again — to ourselves and our competitors.

The political arena is an important place for us to take action. People from American industry spend a huge amount of time and effort buttonholing elected officials and arguing for thousands of individual changes to our tax laws, to our energy policies, to all of the ways in which our government micro-manages our operations and diverts a portion of the wealth that we pump into the economy.

We want to be good citizens. We want to pay fair taxes that provide for the common welfare and security of our country. We want to protect our environment and to create social safety nets for pensioners, the sick and elderly. We also want to continue in business so that we can continue to provide jobs for working families across America. Fair enough?

The NAM report provides a clear wake-up call. We must not file it away and dismiss it as just another piece of "pro-business lobbying." In addition to outlining our self-imposed cost burdens, the report highlights our own government's trade data that clearly show:

- Import "penetration" of U.S. markets in manufactured goods is soaring to record levels — to more than two-thirds of our manufacturing gross domestic product by 2002.
- The top four developing country trading partners with the U.S. are not content to sell us t-shirts and low-end goods. They are positioning themselves to grab increasing U.S. market share in such goods as industrial machinery, telecommunications equip-ment, office machines and transportation equipment. Typically referred to as high value-added products, they generate significant economic benefits for the country that produces them. Right now we still enjoy a strong position in such value-added manufacturing, but it is clear that our competitors are gunning for us.

Our competitors are hungry for this kind of manufacturing. Most of our trading partners, to one degree or another, have built their plans for economic growth on a key strategy: Export as much manufactured goods to the United States as they possibly can. They rightfully understand that a solid strategy for building a strong economy is to manufacture high-value goods and sell them to the broadest possible market. They have a clear vision of how manufacturing multiplies the number of jobs and the spread of wealth throughout the entire economy.

Americans have traditionally prized that same drive and that that same goal to use manufacturing as an economic engine. We didn't need to have it printed in a 400-page government manifesto or painted on a roadside billboard. It wasn't even page one of a formal national policy. We simply harnessed the ambition and ingenuity of the American people and let them flourish in a free society. We wanted to build things with steel and concrete. We wanted to make products that people could use and we wanted to make them better and more cheaply next year than we did last year.

When we burden our businesses with the second highest tax rates of all our trading partners, we simply don't have a forward-looking vision of how to compete and succeed.

American manufacturers must overcome a 5.5 percent disadvantage relative to their foreign competitors when it comes to health care and retirement benefits. When we call attention to such facts we must avoid the circular argument of whether American business "should" or "should not" pay at this level. The point is to recognize that it puts us at a disadvantage in head-to-head competition with countries that want to take our business away from us.

America has not fully come to grips with our self-imposed costs related to lawsuits, or what is called "tort litigation." The American Tort Reform Association reports that the cost of the U.S. tort system had swelled to $210 billion by 2001, or $721 for every man, woman and child. Ask yourself if you have received an economic benefit from this system worth $721 for each member of your family.

Under the banner of tort reform American business has lobbied and argued strongly for our government to bring some restraint and reason to the litigation avalanche. The costs of this nationwide lawsuit binge lop more than 2 percent off our gross domestic product.

Just the *potential* costs of product liability suits can strip our economy of jobs. Cessna Aircraft Company ceased making single engine airplanes in the 1980s and did not resume until the 1990s, when tort reform legislation was passed. The reforms resulted in tens of millions of dollars invested and the creation of more than 25,000 jobs in that industry.

A study by The Perryman Group in Texas reported that legal reforms in Texas during the 1990s drove down potential costs to that state's economy by more than $10 billion and provided tangible economic benefits to Texans, including increased personal income and reduced inflation.

Tort reform provides a good example of how grass roots activism can change the political landscape. In state capitals across the country manufacturers often find lawmakers receptive to their concerns. They often understand the economic impacts of manufacturers and appreciate the significance of manufacturing's "multiplier effect" in their state's economy.

Twenty states passed some kind of tort reform legislation in 2005, ranging from comprehensive tort reform legislation to bills such as those protecting food manufacturers, distributors and servers from frivolous lawsuits related to obesity. The grass roots political work will continue, and the country will continue to see incremental progress and economic gain.

Yet even as tort reforms are proven to deliver significant economic and social benefits, the NAM study estimates that we still hand our foreign competitors at least a 3.2 percent competitive advantage because as a nation we have not yet gotten our tort system under control.

But we have the American corporation under control. Consumer safety, environmental protection, workplace safety— all of these receive intense and exacting scrutiny. In fairness it is important to note that many economic benefits from these regulations flow into our economy. For example, China has not yet begun to reckon fully with the costs of its dead rivers and poisonous air, and corruption of any kind of political system can literally wreck an economy.

A 2001 Small Business Administration study estimated that U.S. manufacturers spent $7,904 per employee to comply with environmental, economic, workplace and tax compliance regulations.

The NAM study reported that the total compliance burden for these areas adds up to $160 billion for American manufacturers, which is equivalent to a 12 percent excise tax on their production. Are there economic benefits from these regulations? Yes. Are there costs? Yes. Do we understand whether they are in balance or out of balance?

We cannot understand that question until we reckon with this part of the equation: If we price our manufactured goods out of the market by over-regulating them then we will ultimately have to close the factories and the mills. It will no longer matter how much it costs to make something in the United States. The market will have made it a moot point.

Economist Jeremy Leonard and the National Association of Manufacturers made a compelling case: We must confront our regulatory burdens, our energy policies, and our system of taxation and we must measure them by a new yardstick. This yardstick must establish whether we are helping or hurting manufacturing.

We should state as a matter of national policy that we will advance United States manufacturing in its domestic market and in every market around the world. Right now our nation's policies are still working at cross purposes. It is time to change that.

Which is why we're making noise.

In the time-honored tradition of our nation, American businesses such as Nucor are increasingly engaged in one of the primary duties of citizenship: We are speaking out. In doing this we become better citizens, which is important, but more important to our workers is that we advance our prospects for long-term success.

For too many years many American business people were comfortable and content to speak mainly with other business people. Then the government's involvement in our business expanded along with its economic impacts. That required business people to get out of our comfort zone and start speaking with politicians and the government power structure on a wide range of issues. We formed industry associations large and small, local and national, and these served us well for speaking both with ourselves and with our representatives in government.

Some businesses are just naturally more gregarious than others, or they are rooted in vast consumer markets, the entertainment industry or other pursuits that just made them comfortable in working the crowd. I was not drawn to steelmaking or the steel industry because of its commanding position in the public arena. Most steel executives don't have much star power, and most are much more interested in selling steel than in selling ideas from a bully pulpit.

But that was back before our country was told it could discard its old-time factories and steel mills and turn itself into a "post-industrial society." That was before we saw one set of rules for this country, another set of rules for China, another set of rules for Brazil and another set of rules for Vietnam: One market — many sets of rules.

The old ways just don't cut it. Time is not on our side. So we continue to band together in trade associations that define our common interests and goals. And we unite many trade associations under larger umbrella groups so that we gain strength from numbers. We continue to be heavily involved in educating and persuading our elected officials.

This is the right thing to do because it is in our best interests, but it is also the right thing to do because self-government only works well when we are actively engaged.

And it is high time we progress beyond this notion that "big business" should sit on the sidelines, speak when spoken to, and pay its taxes. "Big business" has a big stake in good government, and "the little guy" has a big stake in big business — as an employee, as a supplier, as a shareholder, as a service provider, as a merchant in the community.

So now we must take the big view. What in the world must we do to survive in the world? The business world can't just talk to itself any more. We can't just talk to Washington or Raleigh or Little Rock or Austin, if American manufacturing is going to survive through the 21st century.

And it is no longer something as simple as a "tax revolt" here in our own country. We must now be awakened and mobilized to speak out and take action on the entire, interconnected global system. Consider how our trade partners use the various tax systems to create an advantage for their goods versus our goods.

We import more than $1.5 trillion of goods each year, and a fair amount of this comes from trading partners that rebate their country's taxes on those goods when they are exported. The most common example is something called the "value-added tax" which is added to a product when sold in its own country. When that same product is exported to the U.S. then the value-added tax is rebated, which nets out to a lower cost and lower price.

At the same time our goods may be subject to tax when being imported into our trading partner's markets. In the final analysis there are two things our government can do to ensure that our competitors' goods can sell at a lower price than American goods. First, we tax our manufacturers and their products with no thought for competitive impacts. Second, we sit on our hands while our competitors use their tax system (and ours) to make our products artificially more expensive.

Shame on us and on our government if our tax system or our national policies give our competitors an unfair advantage. And shame on us if we sit on the sidelines without getting involved in our government and our nation's policies.

So what do we do about it? We must take a page from Paul Revere. And Alexis de Tocqueville, a 19th Century Frenchman who traveled widely in our young country and observed closely our young republic. His book, "Democracy in America," is a classic. In describing this country, he stated: "The nation participates in the making of its laws by the choice of its legislators, and in the execution of them by the choice of the agents of the executive government; it may almost be said to govern itself, so feeble and so restricted is the share left to the administration, so little do the authorities forget their popular origin and the power from which they emanate. The people reign in the American political world as the Deity does in the universe. They are the cause and the aim of all things; everything comes from them, and everything is absorbed in them."

We are the cause and aim of all things. At Nucor we have taken those words to heart. It is time to awaken our fellow citizens and mobilize more Americans to strengthen manu-facturing. In recent years at Nucor we began something unprecedented in our company's history. We have stepped into the public arena to spark grass roots awareness, concern and action on the issues that confront manufacturing.

From South Carolina to Texas, in the hills of Alabama, the Illinois prairie and the bottomlands of Arkansas we have opened the gates to our mills, rented the halls, cooked the barbecue, raised the big tent and brought thousands together to talk about factories, steel mills and jobs — and to talk about politics, unfair trade practices and our nation's policies.

It's not your usual tent-meeting revival subject, but these aren't usual times. We realized it was time to take an urgent message to a wider audience. It dawned on us that Americans were letting their heritage and their economic security bleed away.

Our fellow citizens have not let us down. Most of our mills are near small towns, yet people have come by the thousands to these town hall meetings. On a warm summer evening in Nebraska the cars were backed up for miles as citizens from all walks of life made the effort to come out and learn about America's loss of manufacturing and how they themselves could help reverse the trend.

In South Carolina we hosted a town hall meeting at Darlington Raceway, the NASCAR track dubbed "Too Tough to Tame." It was a great venue for South Carolinians to come together to tackle tough issues. It was gratifying to see about 4,000 of them in the track's infield, but just as important was the attendance of about two dozen elected officials from the local level all the way up to U.S. Representative John Spratt.

One of the key messages of the town hall meetings has been our call for the involvement of local and state elected officials in manufacturing-related issues. International trade and currency issues have proven to have devastating impacts on states and communities, and it is important for our elected representatives at these levels to realize they have a stake in shaping the policies and direction of our country.

The town hall meetings have been viewed as equally important by Democrats and Republicans.

U.S. Senator Lindsey Graham, a Republican who represents South Carolina, could not attend the Darlington Town Hall because of a Senate vote, but he addressed the meeting through a recorded video. It was important that those attending heard one of our nation's most prominent senators say this: "The threat that we face is that the Chinese government routinely violates trade laws. Fair trade is essential for us to survive in the 21st century. Unfair trade could be the demise of American manufacturing."

An equally prominent member of the Democrat Party addressed our New York Town Hall Meeting just a few months later. Sen. Hillary Rodham Clinton had already joined with Sen. Graham as a founding member of the Senate Manufacturing Caucus when she brought a very important message to the meeting:

"I think it's going to take events like this to draw public attention to the crisis in American manufacturing and to stipulate solutions so that we can move forward in the 21st century with the same kind of positive manufacturing agenda that built America," Sen. Clinton said.

Sen. Clinton's message is being echoed by city councils, county councils and other local government bodies in the communities where we are working to spread our grass-roots message. In conjunction with our town hall meetings these local leaders are passing resolutions on behalf of a strong pro-manufacturing agenda — calling for the necessary reforms and changes to American policy to put our industries back on track and restore job growth to manufacturing. Those resolutions are being heard not only in the local communities but in Congress and the White House.

The harder we work to deliver the message the more we discover that the message is being heard and being acted on by members of both parties. This is good for our country and healthy for our political system.

It is also important that our elected representatives have seen thousands of voters who have listened to the facts, asked good questions, registered to vote, and have subsequently contacted their elected representatives.

Local and national media have been drawn to the events by the size of the crowds, but also by the content and message of the meetings. CNN's "Lou Dobbs Tonight" broadcast a live report from the South Carolina meeting where Correspondent Christine Roman described the meeting as a "remarkable event" and our grassroots campaign as a "bare-knuckle fight." I don't object to such hard-hitting adjectives, because all of us involved in this campaign want to deliver a hard-hitting message.

We are finding willing and hard-working allies along the way. The Metals Service Center Institute in this decade has become an effective leader in awakening business leaders to our nation's desperate need for a pro-manufacturing agenda. The MSCI is a trade association that represents a range of interests from metal producers, distributors, processors and users. While Nucor's town hall meetings have been geared toward grass roots involvement and broad political action, the MSCI has been effective in making business leaders in various sectors of the market aware of what is at stake.

And well beyond the industry groups we are meeting key individuals in communities who are moved by our message and by the plight of workers they know in their communities. Following our town hall meeting in Jackson, Mississippi, a local clergyman issued a public statement calling for support at the meeting and asking the community to make that day "a day of reflection and a day of prayer, a day of action to save the manufacturing jobs on which this community is built."

By now tens of millions of Americans know someone personally who has lost a factory job. They have watched middle-aged parents start over with lower-paying jobs at a time when they must help put kids through college or save for retirement.

Thousands of communities continue to struggle with a gutted economy and shuttered mills. Businesses that were built over generations have been moved from our towns and our country lock, stock and loom — with a speed that astounds us. Industries that employed three or four generations of the same family are gone forever, and with them a sense of place and a sense of security.

The breezy promises of a post-industrial society — where nobody makes anything and we merely push "information" from one place to another — have left millions of American workers displaced and disillusioned.

So as we have taken our message beyond the chamber of commerce banquet hall and the houses of Congress we have found American citizens willing to listen. Beyond just listening, they are increasingly willing to vote and to speak up for American manufacturing. Americans are beginning to comprehend just how big the stakes are for our country. They are beginning to speak to their elected representatives. And their representatives are beginning to understand.

In April, 2005 the United States Senate took a vote on a parliamentary matter to which few people outside Washington paid much attention. Such votes occur every day.

But this one was different. It will prove, we hope, a harbinger.

Senator Graham and U.S. Senator Charles Schumer, a New York Democrat, offered an amendment to a foreign affairs bill. This amendment took dead aim at China's decade of currency manipulation. Essentially the amendment recognized the degree of imbalance that the currency manipulation had created between the Chinese yuan and the American dollar. The amendment called on the imposition of 27.5 percent tariffs on all Chinese products coming into the United States unless China abandoned its currency regime.

The amendment provided for a 180-day negotiation period between the two countries, during which time they would be expected to make progress toward a new currency regime. Tariffs would be imposed if no progress was made in that time. For thousands of people in American manufacturing and other sectors who had been working against

146

this unfair trade practice, the Schumer-Graham amendment was one of the most promising signals to come out of Washington in a very long time.

To us it signaled that the telephone calls, the hearings, the town hall meetings, the one-on-one meetings with officeholders — all of the shoe-leather work of democracy — might just pay off. The Schumer-Graham amendment offered a measure of hope that some in Washington were finally willing to stand toe-to-toe with the Chinese.

As we would expect, a motion was made in the Senate to kill the amendment. Just a few years earlier, or even just a couple of years earlier, the motion to kill this amendment would probably have carried, and it would have been relegated to the legislative bone yard. And a decade ago its death would have been both swift and quiet.

But in the spring of 2005, as jobs continued to be one of our nation's leading exports, something unexpected happened. The United States Senate voted resoundingly to keep the Schumer-Graham amendment alive and kicking. The Senate killed the motion to kill Schumer-Graham by a lopsided vote of 67-33. That vote did not generate the kind of headlines that Social Security generates but it still generated a lot of buzz in the media, and in Washington all of the assumptions about Senate votes and foreign trade had to be recalibrated.

Whether coincidence or not the Chinese government within weeks discontinued the practice of pegging its currency to the dollar and announced that it would float relative to a "basket" of currencies. The government also revalued the currency by only two percent, which was about 38 percent short of its imbalance at that time.

Many in the Congress wanted to give the Chinese time to revalue the currency in small increments and preserve economic stability. Others pushed for more aggressive revaluation and more concrete signs from the Chinese government that the currency imbalance was not just being hidden behind window dressing.

I am not impressed by the Chinese government's first steps. I see it as a calculated political move to buy time and to forestall decisive actions on the part of the U.S. government, including Schumer-Graham. But I take heart that our political leaders are beginning to find the courage for more forceful action on behalf of manufacturing. Political courage, like safety, comes in numbers.

We believe in the American political grassroots. And we believe that ultimately we can persuade political leaders in Washington, Beijing, Tokyo or Moscow that we still mean business. In terms of distance it is still a long haul from Nucor's town hall meetings to the capitals of Asia and Europe.

But messages travel at the speed of light, and as we shed light on these issues in town halls, city halls and legislatures, we can inspire confident action by our own government.

We believe we can renew America's vision of itself as the world's leading manufacturing country. We believe people will respond to this vision and take it as their own. Americans still know this in their hearts. This is who we are. This is what we do. We make things.

CHAPTER 6
THE ANIMAL SPIRITS OF RISK-TAKING

If I want to spark an old-fashioned, bare-knuckle political debate these days I know how to do it with just two words. The first word begins with "S."

"Steel industry" right?

Nope. "Social Security." As a political issue it is in a class by itself. It transcends gender, race, age, Blue State-Red State punditry and most of the usual categories that we slap on people and their politics.

Social Security: The term inspires feelings of comfort (when we think about its intended purpose) or feelings of concern (when we think about it as a fiscal and political time bomb). As a political topic it makes people show up at meetings, buttonhole candidates, write the newspaper, volunteer for candidates, sign petitions and give a sound bite to local reporters without being asked twice.

As a steelmaker and an American manufacturer I would like for the words "steel industry" to spark the same kind of loyalty and political passion. With that in mind I'm going to borrow the words "social security" for this final chapter. I want to weld together the idea of "social security" and manufacturing for two reasons. First, it's an attention-getter, like a sleek car in an ad. Second, the two ideas deserve to be connected. We cannot have one without the other.

We need to consider social security in its broadest sense — the security of our society. And that means the economic security, military security, and something intangible — that sense of security which springs from the American Spirit:

forward-looking, ambitious, can-do. We generate that sense of security when we create economic progress. We lose that sense of security when we shirk our responsibilities to carve out a level international playing field and fail to foster pro-manufacturing policies here in our own country.

There can be no social security in the absence of economic security. Yet, as we enter the 21st century we are exporting both our means of production and our wealth. And the unpleasant truth is that we must shoulder some of the blame.

Consider this one word: Deficit. On this one word hang multiple evils in our current economy. Our federal government's budget betrays our unwillingness to govern responsibly and balance our government spending with revenues. It is measured in dollars, but it demonstrates our lack of discipline. Our lack of political courage in dealing with interest groups and tough issues shifts the burden of debt to citizens who aren't yet old enough to pay taxes and to those not even born yet.

Along with our government's fiscal deficit our trade deficit blatantly undermines our nation's security. It has already been demonstrated to siphon off jobs and productive capacity to countries that are undermining wages, workers rights and environmental protection in a race to the bottom.

But just as damaging, it is helping to siphon off the wealth of our country. We have become the world's largest debtor nation, and we are transferring hundreds of billions of dollars of American wealth to other nations. We have created a "current account deficit" that has sent hundreds of billions of dollars of our wealth to the very nations that are undercutting our manufacturers.

Economists continue to argue the point of whether we are doing our economy dangerous harm. We should not be lulled into a sense of false security by the fact that some economists think our present course is okay. Today in this country economists argue that our budget deficit doesn't really matter, that our trade deficit doesn't really matter and that our current account deficit doesn't really matter.

In 2005, U.S. Federal Reserve Governor Donald L. Kohn said, "We are buying more than we produce, and the extra purchases come from importing more than we export, financed by net borrowing from abroad. The resulting current account deficit has risen to a record level, in excess of 6 percent of gross domestic product."

The United States has become the world's largest debtor nation. We are not only asking our grandchildren for IOUs to cover our government entitlement programs, we are issuing IOUs to some of our fiercest trading competitors. Think of this: Our competitors are using the money that *we* spend on *their* goods to build *their* economies, and enabling *them* become holders of *our* debt. In some cases we are contributing to their military build-up.

Many economists have linked the mid-2000s real-estate boom to interest rates that have been kept low by the massive investment by foreign countries in U.S. debt. As our nation becomes more leveraged we must ask this question: Who has got their hands on the levers of our debt and our economy? It is a question for people concerned about their social security.

151

From 1996 to 2004 our current account deficit ballooned from $120 billion (which was too high) to $666 billion. In the first quarter of 2005 the growth of the deficit continued at a brisk pace, reaching more than $195 billion after just the first three months of the year.

By mid-2005 the Chinese government was sitting on almost three quarters of a trillion dollars in its foreign currency reserves, which had largely escaped the notice of Americans until a largely state-owned Chinese oil company made a strong bid for U.S. oil company Unocal. About that same time another Chinese entity made a public bid for Maytag. Together, those two prospects suddenly put one of our great geopolitical rivals (and trading partner) in a whole new light.

The sudden realization that countries like China can step in and buy American companies with America dollars made some people realize for the first time that some things about our economy are fundamentally out of whack.

Our federal budget deficit shows us to be deficient in discipline and foresight. It also has profound effects on the value of our currency and it can add stimulus to an economy in which we are already spending too much and saving too little. Our trade deficit shows us to be spending too much, and there are other statistics to show that we are saving too little. Our overall deficit within our Balance of Payments shows us that we are entirely too willing to give increasing amounts of our wealth (and control of our wealth) to our competitors.

Add it all up and you get serious questions regarding our nation's financial security.

One of the weak legs in our social security is our growing dependence on foreign energy sources. Enough has been written about our energy appetites and dependence that many people quit paying attention years ago. Please allow me just a couple of thoughts in the wake of the national energy legislation passed by the U.S. Congress in 2005.

Of course it contained something for everyone. Tax credits for buyers of hybrid cars and energy-saving appliances — that got some headlines. Subsidies for ethanol were toasted in the corn states in spite of the fact that the farmers may stand to benefit the least, if at all. Loan guarantees and subsidies for clean energy technology received nods of approval from the green-inclined.

But that is not what grabbed my attention. After more than 30 years of talking and debating and spending billions and billions of dollars on energy — after creating massive government bureaucracies and a cabinet secretary — we still cannot agree on the fundamental wisdom of making our nation more productive and self-reliant in energy.

Hurricanes Katrina and Rita have shown us how we are more vulnerable than ever before to a severe energy shock, at a time when global competition for fossil fuel is escalating to unprecedented levels. Yet several states and their elected representatives were opposed to the United States even conducting a basic inventory of offshore natural gas and oil deposits.

Why? Why would anyone interested in energy security oppose something as fundamental as an inventory? Because if we find oil and natural gas then we might decide it is in our

153

national interest to drill for it, extract it, transport it and use it to fuel our economy.

What a concept.

One of the supposed "breakthroughs" of the Energy Bill was its provisions to make it easier to import liquefied natural gas. From 1998 to 2001 the United States more than doubled its imports of liquefied natural gas from 85 billion cubic feet to 235 billion cubic feet, or about 16 percent of our consumption. Over the next three years imports grew to account for 19 percent of consumption.

Some were praising the Energy Bill's provisions to give the federal government greater power to overcome local opposition to the construction of import terminals for liquefied natural gas. I don't have an argument with importing this energy per se. My point is that we lack a unified, coherent view of how our energy dependence undermines our economy and our economic security. As a result our various states and interest groups work at cross purposes.

We need to make sure that our national policy does nothing to put our nation's own energy resources at an economic disadvantage. One underlying problem with energy is that we have already picked a lot of the low hanging fruit. The U.S. Energy Department reports that two-thirds of all the oil discovered in the U.S. remains in the ground. Likewise we have significant natural gas resources, but the cost to recover these is climbing as we deplete the easier-to-tap resources.

More than 70 percent of U.S. natural gas comes from wells drilled deeper than 5,000 feet. It is estimated that

154

more than 125 trillion cubic feet of natural gas lies at depths greater than 15,000 feet, but the costs of recovering this resource will be significant. It is expected that more than 50 percent of the cost could come in drilling the final 10 percent of these very deep wells.

The government is helping to fund and research new technology to advance deep drilling and other energy extraction, but the government must also make sure that our nation's economic and trade policies deliver reliable, affordable energy to our manufacturing sector.

In 2004 and 2005 when American drivers were feeling pain at the pump, we at Nucor faced a similar hit to the wallet. For each ton of steel produced from second quarter of 2004 to second quarter 2005 the cost of energy shot up 17 percent. It increased 8 percent just from first quarter of 2005 to second quarter. Except for the cost of scrap steel, which we recycle to make new products, our largest cost is energy. Any increase in energy costs poses a serious problem to steel makers. Double-digit increases can quickly make us uncompetitive — or worse. Industries such as ours can suffer serious and sometimes fatal damage if we face energy price spikes that coincide with market surplus and price collapse for our finished products.

The American steel industry would be in a much more secure economic position if we could reduce the political volatility and the price volatility of energy.

The bad news is that we're not much closer to that goal than when I graduated from college and started my steel career. As a result, today's energy markets only add to our social *in*security.

155

In 2003, U.S. Senator Joseph Lieberman from Connecticut addressed the Senate concerning manufacturing and national security. Specifically, he addressed the potential for the United States to lose its strategic advantage and self-reliance in the area of semiconductor manufacturing.

For a generation of Americans who have watched evening news coverage of wars fought with smart bombs and cruise missiles we may take this advantage for granted. But Senator Lieberman sounded a warning in 2003.

In his Senate address Sen. Lieberman said, "The composition of the global semiconductor industry has changed dramatically in recent years. East Asian countries are leveraging these changing market forces through their national trade and industrial policies to drive a migration of semiconductor manufacturing to that region, particularly China, through a large array of direct and indirect subsidies to their domestic semiconductor industry.

"If this accelerating shift in manufacturing overseas continues, the U.S. will lose the ability over time to reliably obtain high-end semiconductor integrated circuits from trusted sources, at a time when these advanced processing components are becoming a crucial defense technology advantage to the U.S."

Senator Lieberman's remarks, and the White Paper on which he based them, illustrate how the progression of market forces, coupled with deliberate and concerted actions by foreign governments, can undermine strategic manufacturing in a relative short time. His intent, Sen. Lieberman said, is for the United States to take actions "to avoid a potential national security crisis in terms of reliable access to cutting-edge technology necessary to the critical defense needs of our country."

What began to happen to the United States semiconductor industry in the 2000s serves as a good example of how international trade can be used as an instrument of government policy to achieve not only an economic advantage but a strategic defense advantage — or to put it another way, to put your competitor at a strategic *dis*advantage.

Sen. Lieberman's White Paper characterized the threat to national security as "imminent" and said that an "accelerating shift in manufacturing overseas" could cost the United States defense establishment the ability to obtain semiconductor integrated circuits from "trusted sources."

The report said this: "If the ongoing migration of chip manufacturing sector continues to East Asia, DoD (Department of Defense) and our intelligence services will lose both first access and assured access to secure advanced chip-making capability, at the same time that these components are becoming a crucial defense technology advantage."

The paper also pointed out that there was much more to this "accelerating shift" than just cheaper labor. It is instructive to see how market forces can be harnessed by anti-competitive government policies to wrestle technology, manufacturing, and a national security advantage away from our country.

The paper cited a slowing in the growth rate of revenues in semiconductor manufacturing. This exerted economic pressure on manufacturers. At the same time the costs of developing and constructing fabrication facilities had increased sharply. On top of these two trends the recession struck, putting a further squeeze on manufacturers.

The Chinese government, in concert with local and regional governments implemented what the White Paper characterized as "a large array of direct and indirect subsidies to support their domestic semiconductor industry."

They also developed partnerships with U.S. and European companies and implemented tax policies to attract foreign capital.

An example of how the Chinese government manipulates its tax system to implement a back-door subsidy is its value-added tax. This has emerged as an all-too-common maneuver in global trade, and it is one that United States manufacturers have fought around the world.

Basically the Chinese government set up a policy to rebate its value-added tax charged on Chinese-made chips. The government provides a 14 percent rebate on this tax to customers that purchase Chinese-made chips, reducing that tax from 17 percent to 3 percent. But U.S.-made chips would still be assessed the full 17 percent tax.

The Chinese government has funded industrial parks, adding to the built-in advantage of lower construction costs in China. The government is actively funding the development of infrastructure to give semiconductor manufacturing a cost advantage in that country. Sen. Lieberman's White Paper also cites China's "apparent disinterest in the expensive pollution controls required of fabrication facilities in the U.S. . . ."

The report goes on to say, "It is therefore important to understand that the current shift in manufacturing capacity

158

to China is not entirely the result of market forces. It is equally important to recognize that even if some residual U.S. manufacturing capacity remains after this large-scale migration takes place, the shift of the bulk of semiconductor manufacturing will severely constrain the ability of the U.S. to maintain high-end research and development."

Sen. Lieberman rightly called on the U.S. government, including defense and intelligence establishments, to focus its efforts on a comprehensive strategy to deal with the trade issues and national security issues. I suggest this would be a healthy perspective for our government to take for all of our manufacturing issues.

The semiconductor industry has been a jewel in the crown of American manufacturing, and it as economic resource that we should protect from any unfair action by every foreign government. In the year that Sen. Lieberman submitted his White Paper the industry employed 226,000 people in this country and accounted for $80 billion in sales, with a 48 percent share of the global market.

At that time the industry was investing about 30 percent of its revenues in the future. But by 2005 only 20 percent of the new state-of-the-art chip making facilities were being constructed in the United States. The government and the people of this country should be very jealous of every dollar of that investment that leaves the United States and every job. And we should never forget that for every dollar and every job that leaves we lose a potential investment in our national security.

George Scalise, President of the Semiconductor Industry Association, wrote this: "Three of the most critical challenges we are addressing pertain to maintaining and enforcing strong trade laws worldwide and enacting enlightened tax policy here at home to ensure America's chipmakers can compete on the basis of their technological capabilities and product offerings."

We don't often associate trade laws and tax policies with national security, but Sen. Lieberman and Mr. Scalise provide a compelling case that all of these are connected. We can draw a key lesson from this industry by looking at the progression of events.

The potential for the industry to move offshore has its roots in market forces. It begins with flattening revenue growth and increased cost pressure. What happens next is that foreign governments intervene and harness these market forces with subsidies and policies that exaggerate an economic advantage — or to put in another way, create an unfair and illegal advantage.

I believe our thinking about "free trade" and "market forces" often suffers from our failure to see how these markets play out. Some will look at the underlying trends of the marketplace and chalk up the offshoring of semi-conductor manufacturing to a "cost-revenue squeeze" or "rising costs of manufacturing in the U.S. compounded by downward price pressures and flattened revenue streams."

If we leave out the parts about "unfair trade practices" and "threats to national defense preparedness and security" then perhaps we have fallen victim to our own free trade myopia. Maybe our habitual way of looking at manufacturing and trade in this country have blinded us to parts of the big picture — the parts that make us more militarily secure, more socially secure.

For years our nation has evaluated its security and its steel industry. The Trade Expansion Act of 1962 requires the Secretary of Commerce to issue a report on the effects of imports of iron ore and semi-finished steel on national security. The 2001 report said that the U.S. in 2000 produced 63.1 million metric tons of iron ore, "far more than the maximum amount needed for national security requirements."

And: "In 2000, the United States produced domestically 112.2 million net tons of semi-finished steel- far in excess of 36.04 million net tons, the maximum required for U.S. national security."

And: "More than 30 countries exported semi-finished steel to the United States in 2000. Brazil and Mexico alone accounted for over 50 percent of these imports. Both countries are safe and reliable suppliers. Brazil is a participant in the Free Trade Area of the Americas initiative. Mexico — with which the United States shares a 1,550-mile border — is a close ally and is a party to NAFTA."

Bottom line, the report says, "Domestic production of finished steel necessary to meet national security requirements is not dependent upon imports of iron ore or semi-finished steel, and in any event, imports of iron ore and semi-finished steel are from safe and diverse suppliers."

Two points I'd like to make: First, to truly ensure national security we can't just "net out" an arbitrary portion of our manufacturing base for "national security." We need to have a healthy manufacturing sector in steel that can do much more than just meet this assigned national security allotment. "National defense" simply cannot provide enough of a market to justify the capital costs. We need a market that is large enough to build and operate a steel industry. We need a steel industry that is large enough and robust enough to keep our overall economy moving and keep it self-reliant in a time of war or global conflict.

My second point does not imply any disrespect or distrust of Mexico or Brazil, but they are competitors, and if push comes to shove in global conflict we may find them more or less "safe and reliable" suppliers — especially if the whole geopolitical cart gets pulled into the ditch.

Call me old-fashioned, but to me "safe and reliable" means "Made in the USA" and in the final analysis of national security we should not compromise on that point.

Ultimately there can be no "social security" in the United States without manufacturing. We depend on it for the basic materials and basic goods of our society. We depend on it for our spears and our plowshares.

Americans must resist the idea of a "post-industrial society." It has infected our thinking and our assumptions about our path to prosperity and security. Our society, our culture and our identity are all built on making things. Manufacturing is the true social security of this nation and we must reclaim it as part of the birthright of our nation.

But in this day and time it is almost as if we are suffering from a national amnesia. We have forgotten and turned away from our heritage. We have lost focus on the fundamentals of our economy and our culture.

We tune out the news stories about fair trade or China's currency policies, and we skip the editorial page to check the box scores or the playoff summaries.

We can't afford any longer to ignore what is going on in the world of politics and trade. We can't afford to tune out the news stories about floods of imports or China's currency policies. We can't afford to sit on the sidelines of the public debate. If we allow a vacuum to form around an important issue or debate, our opposition will fill it. We can't afford to stay home on election day, and we can't afford to ignore what happens to an industry just because we don't work in it.

We can't afford to kid ourselves any more about the economic stagnation that will set in if America loses its critical mass in manufacturing. We can't afford the loss of research and development — with all of its intellectual ferment and innovation. We can't afford to shutter entire towns and communities as we close the factories and mills that constitute their economic life's blood.

We can't afford the flimsy assurances of statisticians who glibly point out that lost manufacturing jobs can be replaced with jobs in "growing sectors" such as "health care." We certainly can't afford to become a nation of hospitals and nursing homes. That is no more plausible than the "information society."

We are teetering on the brink of a massive economic and social experiment. If we are truly, blindly determined to "race to the bottom" in consumer prices, workers' rights, environmental protections and cost of production, then we may be purchasing for ourselves a devil's bargain, in which we ourselves precipitate the massive export of our means of

163

production. Once our economy slides too far down the slope we may find that we can no longer afford to get our country back into a leading economic position.

Thomas J. Duesterberg is president and chief executive officer of the Manufacturers Alliance/MAPI, and Daniel J. Meckstroth is the organization's chief economist. In a 2005 column in *IndustryWeek* magazine, they wrote, "In the face of relentless foreign competition, overzealous regulators and prosecutors, and difficult cost pressures (now magnified by high materials costs), the animal spirits of risk-taking in the manufacturing sector are themselves at risk, as witnessed by historic lows of plant and job creation. Fortunately there are deep reservoirs of optimism among American executives, buttressed by the efficient creative genius of our best innovators and researchers."

I believe they tapped a deep vein in those sentences: "the animal spirits of risk-taking in the manufacturing sector" and "deep reservoirs of optimism." There we are. We still have the spirit and we still possess the optimism.

This is how it is with Americans. Part of the American Spirit has been this "animal spirit" of making things and taking risks. This is who we are. This is what we do. We make things, and we make them as well or better than anyone on earth. And since the days when Paul Revere made brass fittings and copper sheets for American warships we have taught the world how to make things while extending and redefining rights and liberties for workers. We have made things while spending more money to protect the environment than anyone else in the world. When we put the

"Made in USA" label on a product it stands for the people who made it.

There is a satisfaction in this animal spirit. I have seen it more times than I can count in the steel mills where I have worked. I have seen people who do it better than anyone else in the world.

We recognize it when we see it. There is something we have all experienced when we have had the opportunity to watch people making things. As we watch people operate equipment or demonstrate a particular dexterity and skill in making something we feel that certain admiration for their extra measure of competence and confidence.

With all due respect to the evangelists of the "information society" I think they have overlooked something.

The true believers in the information society just don't get it. They just don't get human nature. In order to expand their understanding I would suggest a field trip to Glen Elder, Kansas. It is a small town about halfway between Missouri and Colorado, just a few miles south of the Nebraska border. Glen Elder is the home of Winkel Manufacturing.

Winkel Manufacturing won't show up on the Fortune 500 list. It is a privately-held company, so stockbrokers and mutual fund managers don't have a single word to say about it. But volumes could be written about this company and thousands others like it because they capture that spirit and that optimism that drive human beings to make things.

Paul Winkel grew up the youngest of eight boys so he no doubt needed that spirit and optimism. In describing his company's history he states simply that he "enjoyed welding and making things out of metal."

165

He's my kind of guy — a steel guy. It was in his blood to make things out of steel, so he channeled his hobby and his love of the work into a business. In 1952 he started Winkel Manufacturing to make custom truck bumpers. He expanded the business to make stock racks that could slide into pickup truck beds, portable corrals and livestock feeders. Today the company manufactures truck beds, gates, saddle racks, calving pens and many other essentials for farming and ranching.

It is a family business so the business is in their blood, and their blood is in the business. The Winkels would tell you, "This is who we are. This is what we do. We make things." There is no cubicle in America that would offer the same satisfaction to Paul Winkel. There is no way to stack, sort, shuffle, sift or sell information to make "information age" jobs attractive to the Paul Winkels of the world.

We need to recognize this fact. We need to acknowledge that the steel giants like Nucor and the family-owned manufacturers like Winkel Manufacturing are cut from the same cloth — or more precisely, forged from the same steel. Our people possess the same spirit. And we play on the same field.

The "level playing field" has become a mantra for American manufacturers. It is a term that Americans readily understand and embrace because it is a cornerstone of our democracy, our culture and good business. The level playing field in today's global arena system is not a favor or a request to be granted. American businesses have earned a place of leadership in global business and we are right in expecting the level playing field to be the foundation for international trade and business.

It is our government's responsibility to ensure the level playing field. And it is our responsibility to elect, lead and influence our government's actions in this arena.

We have had our wake-up in this country. The latter-day Paul Reveres are now too many to count. They have sounded the cry in the United States Congress, in the state capitals and in town squares across the country.

We have heard the call from businesses large and small, from labor unions and from millions of displaced workers. We have been warned and urged to action. Our greatest need now is to unify our nation in the conviction that making things must always occupy a place of high honor in this country and that we will spare no effort to keep manufacturing strong.

If that means tough trade negotiations, let's do it. If that means untangling our tax code, let's do it. If that means remembering to respect the factory job, let's do it.

Whatever it takes, let's do it.

We can't afford not to.

Shame on our government leaders if they refuse to provide us with a level playing field on which to compete. Shame on us if we don't demand it of them. Given a reasonably level playing field, shame on us if we can't compete and win.